"석우에게

삼촌으로부터 "

심한구

10th MAY 2000

COMMUNICATION STYLES
IN TWO
DIFFERENT CULTURES:
KOREAN AND AMERICAN

COMMUNICATION STYLES
IN TWO
DIFFERENT CULTURES:
KOREAN AND AMERICAN

Myung-Seok Park
Dan Kook University of Foreign Studies, Seoul

HAN SHIN PUBLISHING CO.
Seoul, Korea

IN COMMEMORATION OF THE INTERNATIONAL EAST-WEST
CENTER ALUMNI REUNION CONVENTION AND SYMPOSIUM:
SEOUL, KOREA, AUGUST 1979

Hanshin Publishing Co.
235-4 Yongdap-dong, Seongdong-gu, Seoul 133-170, Korea

PRINTED IN KOREA

Price: U. S. $ 24.95 (12,000원)

ISBN 89-348-0358-4 (93740)

Preface to Second Edition

Two centuries after the industrial revolution, we have finally reached a stage of development in which modern telecommunication techniques have integrated this earth into a single network of information systems. In a world rapidly shrinking into one small village one feels more than ever the need to establish a firm groundwork upon which cross-cultural communication may be effected successfully. This volume on some socio-cultural patterns underlying two different cultures, Korea and the United States, is a venture to fill such a need. Although far from being definitive, it is one step toward bridging cultural gaps between two remote countries.

The last decade or so has found the Eastern hemisphere to have assumed an increasingly vital role at this stage of internationalization in the world. In particular, since the closing years of the 80's Korea has emerged as an economic power second to the United States of America, aided not only by recent technological advancements, but also by Korean people's unprecedented hard work in every walk of life.

As a consequence, successful cultural communication underlying different cultures of these two countries has been of a major concern, because it often plays a decisive role in cross-cultural decision making by people living in each country. This second edition is my attempt to revise the original publication, accommodating the recent societal changes, as well as my own renewed interpretation of various linguistic and cultural differences.

The overall layout of the first three chapters remains largely as it was, but other necessary changes are substantially made. Three major changes made in this volume merit the readers' attention. The first change occurs in Chapter 1 where I expanded cross-linguistic differences that are found between the Korean and English languages. In so doing, I exemplified as many linguistic differences as possible in language forms, so that layman readers who are not trained in linguistics can come to grips with them. The second change made in Chapter 2 was to update and expand the cultural differences that are adducible between Koreans and Americans. The third change was to replace the Appendix (containing articles contributed by others) with a half dozen of my collaborative writings that appeared in journals over the past ten years or so. These changes will enhance the quality of the present volume, because of its extended coverage of materials in the area of cross-cultural communication. The bibliography and Index have been revised, in accordance with changes made in the volume.

I am very grateful to Dr. Inseok Kim of Brown University, who read the entire first edition and provided the insightful suggestions not only on linguistic differences, but also on enriching cross-cultural differences. My special thanks also go with Dr. Hye-Joon Yoon of Dankook University for his assistance in cross-referencing and indexing.

Myung-Seok Park

1994 Seoul

Table of Contents

INTRODUCTION *

When a foreigner engages in dialogue with people of a host country, he immediately realizes that he has stepped on soil where different patterns of behavior as well as speech prevail. From this moment on, he is likely to regret that his preparation for a trip to this foreign land was not adequate, as he finds that his customary body language is not sufficient to convey his message to those around him, people whose appearance may be quite different from his own. This feeling of regret originates from the breakdown of cross-cultural communication, the success of which depends not only on command of the target language, but also on mastery of the target culture.

The problem in communication between people of different languages and cultures perplexes foreigners, perhaps to the same extent as the gap that exists between them. For example, many American travelers in Korea find themselves surrounded by the Korean language with its monotonous sounds (mechanically regular — a series of little bursts of sound, all of about the same size and force, to use Professor Park's term), especially if they have not been exposed to the language over an extended period of time. This sense of monotony reflects the Americans' habitual experience of the rhythmical tone of the English language, making a sharp contrast to the cacophonic tone of the Korean language. Similarly, many American visitors, no matter how fluent in Korean they may be, tend to be shocked when Korean businessmen pass the same cup they have been drinking from and pour *soju* for them to drink. This cultural shock is caused by

* I am very honored to dedicate this Introduction to my former Professor, Park Myung Seok, who has made me what I am now, since my undergraduate studies in the Department of English of the Hankuk University of Foreign Studies in the late nineteen seventies. His mentorship was so influential during that time and throughout my postgraduate career that I volunteered to write this Introduction in return for all he has done for me.

Americans' lack of understanding of the Korean cultural practice of passing their cup around the table to friends and strangers alike.

The opposite phenomenon can be experienced by Koreans visiting America. The tone of the English language sounds so rhythmical to the ears of Koreans that they mistake it for singing. The fast and seemingly mumbling speech of American speakers exasperates Koreans when they try to decode what they have heard. Many Koreans also tend to find distasteful the sight of an American couple hugging and kissing passionately in public. This sense of reserve may stereotype Koreans as being strait-laced and rigid. Professor Park's book aims to help Koreans and Americans communicate cross-culturally in a foreign context.

He begins the first chapter by illustrating linguistic differences between the Korean and English languages. The premise for presenting linguistic differences lies in his belief that they are inseparable from cultural differences (a theme that will be taken up in the ensuing paragraphs), both of which affect the ways in which users of these languages communicate. Professor Park has identified these linguistic differences as a barrier to effective communication between speakers of two different languages.

Linguists generally believe that English as an Indo-European language stands in sharp contrast to Korean as an Ural-Altaic language in the categories of pronunciation, structure, meaning, and overall flow of information. Consequently, the Korean language is well known to be one of the most difficult languages for English speakers to learn, in and out of the classroom. The difficulty is largely attributed to the extensive and fundamental differences between the two languages, which causes Americans and Koreans to transfer their first language knowledge into their communication in the foreign language. Although we have seen an increasing demand for well-reasoned explanations of those linguistic differences for foreigners who wish to visit or get to know more about Korea, the linguistic analyses they find in most introductory books are often difficult to understand, precisely because they are not aimed at laymen.

Professor Park has attempted to describe and personalize the major linguistic differences in layman's terms. In setting forth the contrasting linguistic presentations, he has avoided as much as possible linguistic jargon to keep non-specialists from being discouraged in reading this book.

He begins by comparing and contrasting the sound systems of Korean and English in which he has identified several problem areas that are encountered by Koreans and Americans. These are nine English fricatives and sibilants (f,v,s,z,θ,ð,∫,ʒ,h), three voiceless stops (p, t, k) for Korean speakers and three unaspirated stops (ㄱ, ㄴ, ㅂ) for English speakers. He has shrewdly observed that both speakers substitute similar sounds for the target ones from their native tongues. Other problems that he thinks make communication very difficult are the differences between English long /iy/ vs. short /i/ vowels, /ɛ/ vs. /æ/, and glides. According to Professor Park, ordinary Korean speakers tend to blur the vowel length, influenced by the Korean vowel /이/, that has an intermediate length. A similar tendency can be found when Koreans mix up English /ɛ/ over /æ/ due to Korean counterparts /에/ and /애/, respectively.

His comparison of the English system of stress and intonation patterns against the syllable-timed Korean language draws much attention in that many Korean speakers are not accustomed to applying any stress or intonation contours on their English, whereas English speakers tend to apply unnecessary stress and intonation on their Korean. Both of these, of course, result in mispronunciation of the target sounds.

At the level of grammatical structures Professor Park also finds insurmountable differences between English and Korean. He notes that the difference in word order makes it very difficult for both speakers to translate Korean sentences into English equivalents and vice versa. He convinces us that the correct use of determiners and prepositions in English poses a persistent problem for Koreans learning English, primarily because of its subtlety in use. He acknowledges that idiomatic expressions and metaphorical expressions are especially vexing for native Korean speakers because they express more than what the combination of the words in sentences would seem to mean collectively. Thus, he concludes that to master idiomatic and metaphorical expressions is of paramount importance to Koreans because "they are at the heart of the English language and provide color, informality, charm, and exactness in daily speech and writing."

The section in which Professor Park deals with emotive meanings should be informative and illuminating to Americans and Koreans alike. The proper use of words or phrases that connote emotive meanings is particularly vulnerable to errors because emotive meanings are the ones that native speakers can adduce from the given word or words through their immersion in the language throughout their life-time. This problem is aggravated by the fact that it is extremely diffi-cult, if not impossible, to achieve one-to-one correspondence between two English and Korean words in use because of intrinsic differences in the cultural backgrounds with which they are imbued. A couple of telltale episodes arising from the misinterpretations of emotive meanings by both speakers, as he recounts, is anything but what one can take for granted.

The second chapter deals with a range of problems that is liable to occur in cross cultural communication between Americans and Koreans at every level. One of the important notions that he thinks underlies these noticeable problems is cultural transfer in which the speaker of one language overlaps his own cultural experience, while assimilating to the other culture. Professor Park says that "in the process of this transfer there must be some degree of distortion and loss," which misguides the participants straddling the cultural fence. At one point he emphasizes that cultural barriers are more difficult to come to grips with than linguistic barriers, although he duly admits the existence of their inseparable relationships.

He covered a wide range of areas in which the expose of Korean culture differs from that of American culture. Very revealing are common threads of cultural matrix that are woven through a number of Professor Park's personal observations and episodes exemplified in the chapter.

The first common thread underlying them is that Korean culture seems to attach more importance to the stative than to the dynamic, whereas American culture does the opposite. According to a school of ancient philosophers, culture is in part molded out of the wholeness of *Yin* and *Yang* philosophy in due proportion. According to this philosophy, the one side of humanity is the *Yin*, comprising the dark, passive and emotional, while the other side is the *Yang*, comprising the light, active and intellectual.

One may hypothesize that American culture as representative of Western culture is bent toward the *Yang* side, whereas Korean culture as representative of Oriental culture is slanted toward the *Yin* side. Professor Park, for example, streamlined seemingly very different ways in which Koreans and Americans exchange gifts among themselves. As he notes, Koreans rarely open up the gift presented and make a comment in front of the giver, regardless of what that comment might be. In contrast, Americans open up the gift and show their delight or surprise (or make a comment, at least) in front of the giver, which is taken as a matter of courtesy. In this case, the no-comment policy of Koreans in receiving gifts apparently runs counter to Americans' vivacious exchange of gifts, which ensures that both the giver and the receiver reveal what emotion they experience by this exchange. Thus, the passive reception of the gift by the former reflects the *Yin* side of Korean culture, while the lively exchange of gifts of the latter betrays the *Yang* side of American culture.

The exemplification of the Dutch treat, or pay-your-own-bill policy, is also subsumable under the *Yin* and *Yang* side of Korean and American culture, respectively. As Professor Park has noted, Korean people battle over the bill, often going to the extreme of engaging in combat over the honor. No doubt winning the struggle of picking up their bill will decrease their cash flow. Nonetheless, the Korean manner of rushing to the cashier to spend their own money has to do with the overt emotion naturally effervescing in their mind, and is nothing more than a reflection of the *Yin* side of Korean culture. On the other hand, Americans tend to maintain their composure when they are on the brink of having cash removed from their pocket. Most Americans obey the inner feeling that all individuals are responsible only for the portion of what they have caused as the result of their behavior, unless they have incurred debts to others from past interactions. The analytic way of thinking is derived from their cultural matrices, one of which is intellectualism. Again, it seems plausible to conclude that the Dutch treat behavior of Americans is related to the *Yang* side of their culture.

By way of contrast, one may find another common thread central to most of the examples of Korean cultural manifestations that are set down in this book: so-called Confucianism. Confucianism is essentially a political philosophy that originated in China. Over the centuries Confucian political ideology came to constitute the basis of the political ideal and to account for the mainstream of pre-modern philosophy in Korea. Consequently, Confucianism exerted a tremendous influence on various facets of Korean history, culture, and social life. In this regard, Professor Park has noted that "Confucian, with its emphasis on relationships, is one of the chief factors that has determined traditional Korean patterns of thought and action." Although Confucianism in Korea not only made a great contribution to the development of Korean culture, it also produced some serious evils, inevitably deterring the process of modernization in Korea, despite Western influence. Representative of the Confucianization process he amply exemplifies in Chapter 2 are Koreans' preference for sons, age-conscious relationships, male-oriented society, in-group oriented interpersonal interaction, to mention only a few.

Concluding the second chapter, he emphasizes that cultural discrepancies between Koreans and Americans should not allow them to inhibit their cross-cultural communication, no matter how irrational they might be. He instead envisions that "cross-cultural communication should be carried on on the individual merits rather than on vague impressions or prejudices," that may result from the communicants' ignorance of each other's culture.

Chapter 3 deals with patterns of universal behavior across different cultures, regardless of race and nation, that can be often overshadowed by superficial differences. People, for example, have the same facial expressions for such emotions as anger, fear, or sadness. To be more specific, it is not uncommon to notice that, regardless of where they live, people express their anger by not only lowering their brows with tensed eyes, but also by slightly pressing their lips together. As Professor Park alleges, the "neurophysiological elements corresponding to fear, disgust, anger, or happiness" are characteristic of all people, but differences lie only in what causes them to be angry and, moreover, in how they deal with his anger.

Another universal behavior every culture subscribes to, he says, is "display rules" that are unique to the target culture under examination. For example, in Korea the social taboo of refraining from expressing feelings overtly by kissing in public extends even to the bride and groom during the marriage ceremony, whereas Americans find no reason to repress their feelings. However, it is not hard to imagine that the Korean couple would wear a happy smile and kiss at last, when finally left alone in a private room after the ceremony. The difference boils down to the cultural display rules that substantiate superficial differences between Korean and American couples in that the couples of both cultures are conditioned to the universal behavior of smiling, or at least an impulse to smile, although this behavior may arise at different times.

By the same token, Professor Park holds that the concept of underlying human similarity applies to linguistic differences that often constrain, to a large extent, communication among people of different cultures. Much research by modern linguists focuses on the universal nature of languages in the categories of syntax and semantics. As to syntax, all languages employ some limited number of parts of speech (such as noun, verb, adjective, adverb, etc.), a certain kind of word order (subject-verb-object, subject-object-verb, etc.), forms of sentences (such as statement, question, request, command, interjection, etc.), to list only a few elements of grammar. Evidence for semantic similarities can also be found in that all languages are composed of similar ranges of semantic fields, such as color terms, kinship terms, degree terms, etc. and polarity terms such as large-small, cold-warm, up-down, etc.

Very insightful is Professor Park's conclusion that it is not human nature, but only superficial customs and attitudes that condition us to develop the different behaviors that are reflected in different cultures. As he states, we are all human beings who feel the same emotions and strive at the same comforts and knowledge that make our life so worth living. This conclusion signifies our humanistic approach in communication where each individual must assimilate with reciprocal understanding and preparation into the thought patterns of any new society he may confront. The message Professor Park sends to readers is that no matter how hard it might be to master a foreign language and culture, a person with acquired linguistic knowledge and cultural enrichment is sure to enjoy the feeling of reward by maintaining amicable communication with people of another country. This inevitably will lead to mutually beneficial communication in which all participants are likely to take pride.

Included at the end of the book is a collection of Professor Park's seven collaborative articles that were published in the journals of communication in recent years. Central to the themes of first five research articles are cultural differences in the behavior of Koreans and Americans, ranging from tactile avoidance, world view, and self-monitoring, human values, and patterns of communicative behavior. The other two deal with comparing Korean oral communication patterns and communication apprehension with those of Americans, Swiss, and Japanese. One may note that these studies of his make a great departure from the vein of his previous writings in that they are not only experimental in design and statistical analysis, but also well focused on proving specific inquiries under investigation.

A thorough reading of this book is likely to be much needed for those who wish to deepen their understanding of American and

Korean cultures. As the world has witnessed the emergence of Korea as an equal partner with the USA in the wake of the political and economic autonomy acquired by Asian and Pacific countries, this kind of introductory book, full of insights and nuggets of wisdom, will no doubt serve as an excellent guide for facilitating communication between Koreans and Americans, no matter where that communication may take place.

Andrew-Inseok Kim
Brown University

Chapter 1

CROSS-LINGUISTIC PROBLEMS

This chapter aims at presenting some socio-cultural patterns underlying two different cultures: Korea and the United States, along with some of their cultural as well as linguistic problems or difficulties arising from different communication styles. It illustrates that not only a linguistic competence of the languages concerned but also a thorough grasp of the socio-cultural back-ground of the target languages makes successful communication possible.

Several years ago I came to the University of Hawaii as an East-West-Center grantee for further study. Having nothing particular to do in the evening on the day I arrived, I went to the room specially reserved for the TV set. The room was uncomfortably crowded with American students watching a comedy. At times all the audience broke up and shook the place with the thunder of their mirth. I laughed along not because I found the play irresistibly funny but because I felt that I had to just out of courtesy for the courting couple sitting next to me, who threw their heads back convulsed with whole-hearted laughter. Their laughter was so infectious that I did not want to seem like a wet blanket. The comedy, which was so hilarious to the rest of the people, was but a tragedy to me. I left the room feeling as if I was a helpless child in a strange land. It was still a riddle to me what caused that uncontrollable outburst of laughter.

The man and the women on TV spoke so fast that I could not catch on to all of what they said. Even though I understood some of what they were saying, it did not sound to me like something to be laughing about. Having taught English for many years in Korea, I suddenly realized that I was confronted with cultural as well as linguistic problems.

I will proceed to take a brief view of some of the linguistic differences of the two languages and then examine how the socio-cultural patterns underlying two different cultures pose baffling problems to cross-cultural communication.

Learning a foreign language is really a difficult job. It becomes far harder when the languages are remote from each other in their structures and backgrounds, like English and Korean. The difficulties to be overcome range from phonological to lexical, grammatical, and discoursal forms.

1.1. CONSONANTS AND VOWELS

The sound system of English is so different from that of Korean that a Korean speaker of English encounters a host of English phonological pitfalls. Witness these, for instance. English fricative sounds seem to present one of the most difficult pronunciation problems. Of the nine English separate elements (phonemes) /f,v,s,z,θ,ð,ʃ,ʒ,h/ only two fricatives /s/ and /h/ exist in Korean. Consequently, Koreans often substitute stops and other sounds which they have in their sound system for them. The closest approximations to the English /f/ and /v/ from the sound system of Korean are /p/ and /b/ or their varieties. The Korean learner of English substitutes what is for him an easier sound for a harder sound so that a "cup of coffee" is likely to come out as a "cupo coppee." In the next fricative series, /θ/ and /ð/, the Korean speaker again substitutes similar sounds from his native tongue. He often says "sank you" or "I sink so" or "Is dis what you want?" when attempting to say "thank you," "I think so" or "Is this what you want?" The English /z,ʒ,dʒ/ are three separate elements, but Koreans lump them all into a vague /dʒ/ sound. "Zoo" is pronounced like "Jew".

I recall that a Korean student studying in the United States was once in an awkward predicament because he could not make himself understood. One morning he went to a restaurant and wanted to have a pizza. Unable to distinguish the difference in pronunciation between "pizza" and "pitcher," he said something like "pitcher." He thought he ordered pizza, but much to his chagrin, a huge pitcher full of beer was placed on his table. He later grumbled to his Korean friends that he had to fill his empty belly with that "damned" beer, which he neither ordered nor had the least inclination to drink.

English fricatives and sibilants are a particularly interesting source of trouble for Koreans. As for words ending in, /s,z,ʃ,ʒ,dʒ,tʃ/, some superfluous vowel is usually attached. In Korean no word ends with sounds like these. Words like "shirts" and "inch" borrowed from English are spelled in Korean, 샤쓰 and 인치. Such superfluous vowels can be removed by practicing letting the final consonant just fade away, rather than making it end abruptly.

A Korean speaker has to learn to distinguish voiced and voiceless consonants in English, especially the homologous pairs, such as [p-b, t-d, k-g]. In Korean voiced consonants are only positional variants of corresponding voiceless ones: a consonant is voiced when it comes between other voiced sounds (in "간밤에", [ㅂ] is voiced) but is voiceless in all other positions (in "밤마다", [ㅂ] is voiceless). When a Korean speaker pronounces "박", a native speaker of English invariably writes down "park" (or "pak"), not "bark." In English, voiced and voiceless consonants occur in the same positions (pet:bet): they are not positional variants of each other. A Korean speaker tends to use a voiced consonant instead of a correct voiceless one between voiced sounds: for example, "Pick up" is often pronounced like "pig up." "My back is aching all over" is heard like

"My bag is aching all over." He also tends to use voiceless consonants instead of a correct voiced consonant in other positions: for example "big" is often pronounced like "pick." It can easily be seen that both of these tendencies to err have as their source the Korean language habit of automatically using voiced consonants in certain positions and voiceless consonants in certain other positions.

The English voiceless stops [p, t, k] pose certain problems because of the different varieties in which they occur in different positions. A Korean speaker tends to use one variety, the aspirated one, in all positions. The slightly aspirated varieties at the beginning of a word give no problem, but the unaspirated ones after [s], and between a strong-stressed vowel and a weak-stressed vowel (like "happy", "city", "water") are usually substituted by the aspirated variety and so is the word-final one, which is generally an unreleased variety. Thus although the four [p] sounds in "past", "speak", "happy" and "group" are all phonetically quite different, the average Korean speaker pronounces them all the same.

By the same token, the Korean voiceless stops ㄱ, ㄷ, ㅂ present similar kind of problems for English speakers learning Korean as a foreign language, because they tend to carry over aspiration which occurs in an initial position of the English phonetic system. Thus, they mispronounce 갈, 달, 발 as 칼, 탈, 팔, respectively.

Of the three voiceless stop consonants in English, [t] probably is more difficult for the Korean speaker than the other two. The [t] in a word like "city" or "water" (between strong stressed vowel and weak-stressed vowel) and the [t] that is used in such words as "mountain", "Britain" pose baffling problems for Koreans. The [t] in "city" is not only voiceless and unaspirated but also its articulation is also peculiar, for it is just a single flap of the tongue. Koreans mistake this for a kind of [d] sound, because [d] in this position is pronounced just the way [t] in "writing" is pronounced like "riding" by many native speakers. The [t] before syllabic [n] is also usually aspirated by students. This [t] is pronounced by native speakers without any release at all. The tongue stays on the same point and the air is released through the nose to produce the effect of the syllabic [n̥].

In addition to individual consonant sounds, combinations of consonants cause even worse trouble. English has a great variety of consonant clusters. Two or more consonants stand together without any vowels in the same syllable, so that a Korean speaker is very likely to insert superfluous vowels by pronouncing the letter "e" in "changed" or to insert /ə/ between "would" and "n' t" in pronouncing "wouldn' t" (The same is true of "didn' t."). It is extremely difficult for Korean speaker to read the following stanza at a normal speed:

> Amidst the mists and frozen frosts
> With stoutest wrists and loudest boasts
> He thrusts his fists against the posts
> And still insists he sees the ghosts.

On the other hand, the Korean language has very few types of consonant clusters and these are quite simple ones. When different consonants come together in a Korean word as a result of word formation, the consonants follow certain rules of assimilation. For example, the final[ng] of [tʃong](종) plus the initial [l] of [lo] becomes [ngn] with the[I] assimilating with the [ng](Lukoff 1963: 10). Koreans have therefore a natural tendency to simplify certain combinations of consonants in English. They say "local lews" for "local news", "all light" for "all night." "Equipment" is pronounced like "equimment" or "well-known" is pronounced as "well-lown."

English vowels present no less difficult problems to Korean speakers of English. Take these examples. Korean vowels are generally tense, whereas English vowels are generally on the lax side. The Korean speaker tends to make all English vowels uniformly short and tense, so that confusions like made-mate, bag-back persist. He fails to make vowels somewhat longer before voiced consonants. English vowels are also characterized by diphthongization, the difference, for example, between "live" and "leave" or between "full" and "fool." The Korean speaker either leaves out the diphthongal glide

[y] or [w] or pronounces the diphthong as if it were two distinct vowels. He cannot hear this glide and so cannot tell the difference between the vowel [i] as in "sit" and the diphthong [iy] as in "seat" and in reproducing both [i] and [iy] he tends to use Korean [i] (이), which gives an in-between effect. A native speaker of English cannot tell whether the Korean speaker has said "it" or "eat." English /ɛ/ and /æ/ are lower than Korean counterparts /에/ and /애/, respectively. This means that it is hard for the Korean speaker to distinguish English "pet" from "pat," and, in turn, in his reproduction of English /ɛ/ and /æ/ he either uses a sound close to his Korean / 에/ for both cases or else randomly mixes up /ɛ/ and /æ/, so that "pen" and "pan" may be made to sound alike. A Korean speaker has also a strong tendency to leave out the [y] of "year" or the [w] of "woman."

THE RHYTHM OF KOREAN

THE RHYTHM OF ENGLISH

1.2. RHYTHM PATTERNS

English has peculiar stress and intonation patterns. Stress is put on a syllable of an English word when it is pronounced with such force as to give it more importance than the surrounding syllables and to make it stand out among them: for example, the *par* of "apparently" [əpǽrəntli]. Persons who learn English as a second language often make the mistake of pronouncing unstressed vowels the way they are spelled. In their anxiety to make themselves understood, they will probably be tempted to say [æpǽrɛntli]. Actually, there will be less danger of their being misunderstood, and their English will sound much more natural, if they will obscure the unstressed vowels when pronouncing them. Conversely when a native speaker of English is asked to pronounce "사람" (person), he will usually say [sǽrəm] or [sərám].

The Korean speaker of English has difficulty in understanding those differences of stress that have the power to distinguish meanings. For example, the difference of meaning between, "They are râcing hórses ," and, "they are rácing hòrses," is very great: the first one means that someone is running horses against one another and the other means that they are horses for racing. The ambiguity of the surface structure underlying two meanings is solved by introducing two different stress patterns. These kinds of examples are legion. A gîrl húnter (a girl who hunts) is never a gírl hûnter (a man who hunts girls). The meaning of the sentence, "I have instrúctions to leave" (I am to leave instructions) is quite different from that of the sentence, "I have instructions to léave" (I have been instructed to leave). The sentence "I suspect that you were right thére" means "I suspect that you were there on the spot," whereas the sentence, "I suspect that you were ríght there" means "I suspect that you were right in that matter." At times the difficulty of English stress patterns causes ambiguity to both Americans and Koreans. A sentence like, "We enjoy entertaining visitors," can be interpreted in two ways: one is that we enjoy visitors who provide us entertainment, and the other is that we like to entertain visitors.

The stressing of syllables goes beyond words. We do not really talk in words, most of the time, but in sentences, or at least phrases. In the sentence, "I' ll meet you tomorrow," sentence-stress falls on the syllable which normally receives word-stress: "I' ll méet you tomórrow." In English the high pitch normally coincides with the last sentence-stress as in "The situátion is in tólerable." The native speaker of English sounds awkward and unnatural to Koreans when he utters the Korean sentence placing the high pitch at the end of a sentence as in "나는 사과를 좋아합니다" just the way the English sentence "I like an ápple" is pronounced.

There is a great deal more difference between stressed and unstressed syllables in English than in most other languages: this is as true of sentence-stress as of word-stress. To an English-speaking person the rhythm of many other tongues like Korean, Japanese or Spanish sounds mechanically regular—a series of little bursts of sound all of about the same size and force, like machine–gun fire. In a language like Korean, a sentence is usually determined by counting the total number of syllables, stressed and unstressed alike. Sentences containing the same number of syllables are felt to be of the same length. This is why Korean is called a syllable-timed language. Speaking the Korean language is something like producing a line of soldiers of very much the same size and following one another at rather regular intervals. English pronounced with such a rhythm would probably not be understood.

In a sentence of English, the number of sentence-stresses is more important than the number of syllables. The English language might be pictured as a series of family groups, each made up of an adult accompanied by several small children of varying sizes. A few of the adults might be childless, and some would be larger than others. Here are two lines from Tennyson which are perfectly matched and of the same length:

> Bréak, bréak, bréak,
> On thy cóld gray stónes, O Séa!

Rhythmically speaking, the unstressed syllables are so unimportant that it is not even necessary to count them. When you read those two lines, it takes you as long to say the first as the second, although the first has only three syllables and the second consists of seven, English is indeed a stress-timed language.

English words are usually divided into two classes: *content words*, which have meaning in themselves, like "mother", "forget", and "tomorrow"; and *function words*, which have little or no meaning other than the grammatical idea they express, such as "the", "of", and "will." In general *content words* are stressed, but *function words* are left unstressed, unless the speaker wishes to call special attention to them.

Content words, usually stressed, include nouns, verbs(not auxiliary verbs), adjectives, adverbs, demonstratives like "this", "that", "these", "those", and interrogatives like "who", "when", "why", etc. *Function words* usually unstressed, include articles like "a", "an", "the", prepositions like "to", "in", personal pronouns like "I", "me", "he", "him", "it", possessive adjectives like "my", "his", "your", realtive pronouns like "who", "that", "which", common conjunctions like "and", "but", "that", "as", "if", auxiliary verbs like "be", "have", "do", "will", "would", "shall", "should", "can", "could", "may", "might", "must", and one used as a noun-substitute, as in the red dress and the blue one.

English accents tend to recur at regular intervals. The more unstressed syllables there are between accents, the more rapidly and indistinctly they are pronounced. Pronouncing at normal speed the two sentences like "The boy is interested in enlarging his vocabulary." and "Great progress is made daily.", a native speaker of English unconsciously crushes together the unstressed syllables of the first sentence in order to get them said in time, and he lengthens somewhat the stressed syllables of the second so as to compensate for the lack of intervening unstressed syllables (Prator, 1957:25).

English is an iambic language and favors an alternation of weaker with stronger stresses. Here are two different stanzas from James Thomson and Thomas Gray:

> Gíve a mán a pípe he can smóke
> Gíve a mán a Bóok he can réad;
> And his hóme is bríght with a cálm delíght.
> Though the róoms be póor indéed.

> Fúll mány a gém of púrest ráy seréne
> The dárk unfáthom' d cáves of Ócean béar:
> Fúll mány a flówer is bórn to blúsh unséen.
> And wáste its swéetness on the désert áir.

This is true to a large extent even when you carry on a daily conversation. In a sentence like, "In an hóur it will be réady to turn óver to you," the unstressed syllables are so unimportant, rhythmically speaking, that it is not even necessary to count them. The more unstressed syllables there are between accents, the more rapidly and indistinctly they pronounced.

A native speaker of English gives an impression to a Korean that he speaks too fast, mumbling because he unconsciously crushes together the unstressed syllables. For example, the meaning of the sentences like, "I have two fish", and, "How many guests will you have to feed?" is ambiguous to a Korean speaker of English when they are actually pronounced in everyday living English. When the sounds are in contact with adjoining stream of speech, a change of meaning is likely to occur. The sentence "I have two fish" can be heard as "I have to fish". The response to the question, "How many guests will you have to feed?" can be made, according to your pronunciation, either as, "I have five guests to feed," or as, "I have to feed five guests."

One of my friends working for an American company complained to me that Americans talk too fast and mumble too much. He confided to me that when he was interviewed by an employer, who started to say, "How are you?" he said, "I' m 32 years old", thinking that he was asked, "How old are you?" My friend was further asked, "How long can you stay here?" He answered, "One month," thinking he was asked, "How long have you been here?" When he came to see the employer the next morning, the employer said, "I can' t hire anyone who can only stay here for a month."

1.3. GRAMMATICAL DIFFERENCES

Korean and English, are so different in structure that not only should word order be converted, subjects turned into objects, nouns into verbs, but also in most cases the wording itself must be changed. As the Korean language is structurally very distant from English, there is little formal correspondence. Kim (1989) portrays a mirror-image principle occurring within the framework of word-order classification, and contrasts Korean and English with respect to the features which yield opposite branching directions. According to his principle, the conceptual chunks of English (an Subject-Verb-Object language) are expanded to right-branching clauses such as multiple sentences, complementation (*that* clause), and coordination (*and* clause), whereas those of Korean (an Subject-Object-Verb language) are to the left-branching clauses. This grammatical difference is captured as in the following diagram:

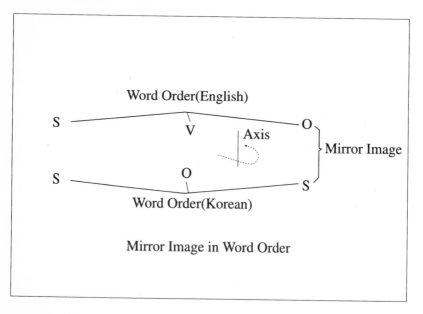

Mirror Image in Word Order

In the diagram, a mirror image is produced when a mirror axis projects Verb-Object in English into Object-Verb in Korean, with the subject held constant.

The mirror image phenomenon, evidenced in Kim's study, can be a major obstacle to Koreans learning English as a foreign or second language, and to Americans learning Korean. As Kim has shrewdly observed, this is because a branching direction is a parameter that has to be reset in the course of the learning experience, because English and Korean stand typologically opposite in this respect. Kim thus conjectures that such a cognitive operation involves heavy memory constraint and a delayed learning process, since English and Korean speakers have nothing in their language experience to guide them.

Verbal communication problems may also stem from the learners' ignorance of prefabricated patterns and co-occurrence restrictions between the two languages. Take these examples. The sentence form, "Nixon is sixty years old," is the response to the question, "How old is Nixon?" Then what is the question form of the sentence regarding the ordinal status of Nixon, "Nixon was the 37th President of the United States?" The desirable question form would be, "How manyth President was Nixon?" (닉슨은 몇째 대통령이었습니까?) as in the case of the Korean question form. There being a pattern hole like this in English, one has to resort to extensive paraphrasing such as "Was Nixon the 37th president of the United States or what?" and, "How many presidents preceded Nixon?" (Song 1975: 25). English is helpless here, whereas Korean can fill the pattern hole neatly. For the English expression, "Please let me know the results of my English test a few days in advance of my departure," a Korean speaker of English would say, "Please let me know the results of my English test in a few days' advance. Co-occurrence restriction occurs at the level of word, phrase or sentence. A native speaker of English is in the habit of associating words in paired cliche's, using "and," "or," "as," and "like." Some of the examples are: "north and south," "room and board," "cup and saucer," "comb and brush," "sticks and stones," "aches and pains," "rain or shine," "friend or foe," "hit or miss," "busy as a bee," "cool as a cucumber," "drinks like a fish," "sells like hotcakes" (Song 1972: 41). All these cliches are so culture-sensitive that both the choice and ordering of the lexical items are culturally determined. Thus the Korean equivalent for "north and south" is "south and north" (nam-puk) (Song 1975: 40). In the examples given above there are no exact equivalent in Korean for pairs like "comb and brush," "cup and saucer," "sticks and stones," "aches and pains," "cool as a cucumber," "drinks like a fish," etc.

The words "pretty" and "handsome" are another example of a similar vein which signifies the restriction that the meaning of a certain word or its associations (the word acquires in a context) tend to co-occur with another given word sharing a common ground. These two words are synonymous in the meaning "good-looking", but may be distinguished by the range of nouns with which they are likely to co-occur (Leech, 1990):

The notable differences in comparing the collocative associations

	English	Korean		English	Korean
	girl	소녀		boy	소년
	boy	*소년		man	남자
	woman	여자		car	*자동차
	flower	꽃		vessel	*배
Pretty	garden	정원	Handsome	overcoat	*코트
(예쁜)	color	색깔	(잘생긴)	airliner	*비행기
	village	마을		typewriter	*타자기
	etc.			etc.	etc.

of English and Korean words referring to "good-looking" are twofold. On the one hand, one may notice that the English words "pretty" and "handsome" are both acceptable for some words (i.e., car, typewriter, etc.), although they suggest a different kind of attractiveness because of the collocative associations of two adjectives. Obviously, gender marked words must select "pretty" over "handsome" or vice versa. Korean, on the other hand, forces the word " 잘생긴(handsome)" to co-occur with a certain type of words, while it allows the word "예쁜(pretty)" to co-occur with a wider range of words.

The difference of this sort stemming from co-occurence restrictions on collocating words hampers the speakers of these two languages in their communication with each other. This difference turns out to be more detrimental to mutual communication than one may think, because the mastery of the collocation rules is not likely to be achieved until many years of learning a foreign language, or probably may require one's life time exposure to it.

The stupendous array of determiners (articles, possessives, qualifiers, etc.) and prepositions in English are extremely vexing and perplexing problems for Korean speakers of English. A noun in English

---

* An asterisk refers to the ungrammaticality of words.

has to appear either with or without one or the other of the articles or one of the other determiners. For instance, "English literature" has no definite article whereas "the English language" has a definite article for no particular reason. One of the most delicate categories in English is the determiner. I will take up the subtle use of the determiner system in English in the lexical section, because it relies heavily on semantic use.

Many mistakes Korean people make when they speak English come not only from their lack of correct knowledge of English prepositions but also from their Korean language habits. They add superfluous prepositions to the following expressions like: "I discussed (about) the matter with him," "Don' t address (to) me as doctor," "He excels (over) all of us in tennis," "Seoul exceeds (over) Pusan in size and population." A noun in English has to be either singular or plural. Singular or plural is optional for the Korean language but for the English language it is obligatory. For the English sentence, "This is a place for children to play," a Korean equivalent, "This is place for child to play" (여기는 아이가 노는 곳입니다.) sounds un-English. The idea of plurality indicated by the repetitive use of a plural noun in the following English sentence cannot be carried over intact to Korean: There are books about books about books.

No less complex are such obligatory categories as gender, number and person if human. A third person singular pronoun in English has to be male, female or neutral. A verb in English, if in the present tense has to reflect the number of the subject. Such a simple term as "saram" (사람) in Korean (the human being in general) can be expressed as man, woman, girl, boy, person and so on. Song (1975) says that the problem of obligatory categories is perhaps more intractable than that of co-occurrence restriction in translation.

1.4. LEXICAL DIFFERENCES

The study of meaning of words is central to the study of human communication; and as communication becomes more and more a crucial factor in social organization, the need to understand it becomes more and more pressing (Leech, 1990).

Meaning is by far the most unstable element in any language. Much difficulty is involved in carrying over from one culture to another an infinite variety of logotactic, contextual, and empirical meanings rendered through an infinitude of surface structures. The English term "rice" denotes successive stages of Korean rice: "rice seedling" (mo), "rice plant" (pye), "unhulled rice" (pye), "hulled rice" (ssal), "glutinous rice" (chapssal), "non-glutinous rice" (moypssal), "rice grains" (mikok), "steamed rice" (pap), etc. (Song 1976:95).

Another such example can be found in an English word "wear"

that is used to denote putting any type of articles (i.e., clothes, hats, footweares, etc.) on human body parts. On the other hand, the Korean language employes a list of words that can be equal in meaning to the English word "wear", depending upon the type of articles one has to put on: "쓰다" (for hat and glasses), "입다" (for clothes), "신다" (for shoes and socks), "끼다"(for ring and gloves), "차다" (for watch and earrings), etc. This phenomenon is convergent because the referents of two or more words in Korean are represented by one single word in English. On the other hand, the opposite phenomenon—so called divergent phenomenon—duly occurs when a single Korean word diverges into a large number of English words. Korean, for example, uses a word "컵" to denote a small open container usually having a handle and used chiefly as a receptable from which to drink tea, soup, etc. regardless of its raw material, whereas its English counterpart words vary depending on what it is made out of : glass (made of transparent plate), mug (made of china), paper cup (made of paper), etc.

Another example that signifies such a divergent phenomenon is the English word "chair" which has a broader semantic space than its counterpart in Korean. The English "chair" has extensively figurative meanings, such as, "a principal academic post in a university," "to preside over," and so on, whereas the Korean word for chair "uyja" (의자) has a very narrow semantic space. The Korean word "uyja" has no figurative meanings whatsoever. It is used only as a device for resting the buttocks or the back when sitting (Song 1975: 27). Conversely the Korean term "chata" (to sleep) seems to be more generic than its English equivalent: in Korean not only animate beings but also inanimate beings sleep, for example, "The wind is sleeping," "The watch is sleeping," "The playing card is sleeping" and so on (Song 1976: 107). The learning of divergent differences seems to be more difficult for Koreans learning English to overcome than the learning of convergent differences, since in the former case Koreans must make a selective response in using an English word, while in the latter case all they have to do is to interpret their meaning in context.

A certain lexical unit is used more frequently and familiarly in one culture than in another. I was once told that Korean workers in the United States have a lot of difficulties understanding certain lexical terms. Take the following for instance. Those who work in hospitals and factories are always asked, "Are you available for all shifts?" Never having heard the word "shift" which is not so frequently used in Korea as it is in the United States, they usually answer in the negative (Workmen in Korea do not have shifts so often as they do in the United States.). Thus they do not succeed in getting the job. Later they understand with surprise that there are different "shifts" in English, for example, hours of "day shift," "swing shift," and "graveyard shift."

The classification of any linguistic unit depends entirely upon the way in which the unit functions within a particular context. No word has exactly the same meaning twice as Hayakawa (1939: 60) put it. For example, "stone" is a noun in, "John threw a stone at me," a verb in, "The angry crowd will stone him to death," and an adverb in the expression, "He is stone deaf." A Korean speaker of English is not usually familiar with the notion that lexical units in English have relatively large potential domains. One final lexical difference that hinders a Korean speaker of English communicating with Americans is the notoriously subtle use of the English determiners (definite and indefinite articles "the, a/an") which Korean lacks. The contrastive use of these two words is clearly manifest in English. Notice, for example, that 'Where's a cat ?' is not the same with 'Where's the cat?' Let's suppose that a husband asked his wife, "Where's the cat?," he took it for granted that his wife whom he is addressing is aware of which cat he is talking about. Both of them know that they have only one cat in their house. If they have more than one cat, or if the husband is talking to someone in the office, the reference to the cat may not be clear. In this situation, more information will be needed for clarification of the referent of the cat. Thus, the use of the definite article hinges on shared knowledge between the speaker and hearer.

The following diagram may visually explain the importance of contextual knowledge that ought to be shared by the speaker and hearer :

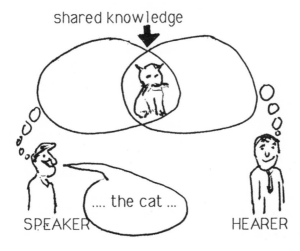

In contrast, when one asks 'Where' s a cat?' , the referent of a cat is not specified and it may refer generically to any small feline pet that can be found at home. We can visualize it as follows:

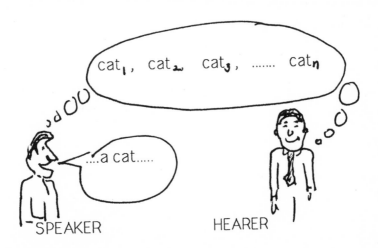

However, the referent of *a cat* can be made specific when it is replaced by the cat in a run-on sentence. For example:

> "They bought *a cat* from the animal hospital;
> but after keeping *the cat* for quite a while,
> they decided to send *the cat* to the orphanage."

The referent of *the cat* is made clear by the fact that *a cat* has already been mentioned earlier in the sentence. Again, as with the definite article, shared contextual knowledge rests on the relationship where *a cat* is coreferential to *the cat*.

For the differential use of these two articles, Leech concluded that the decision to use *the* rather than *a* is a matter of appropriateness to situation. Moreover, the reference of *the X* may change from one situation and another (Leech,1990). There are other kinds of usage of the definite article which include plural phrases such as the children, the flowers, the novels (used for a unique set of referents) and the sun, the president, the moon, etc. (used for only one possible referent).

All these differential usages of the English articles stupefy a speaker of Korean who is trying to communicate with English speakers because of their subtleties.

1.5. DISCOURSAL DIFFERENCES

Whenever we try to deal with language in terms of words, isolated from discourse, serious difficulties inevitably arise, for it is only in the context of the discourse that many potential ambiguities are actually resolved. These difficulties are in fact aggravated when a Korean learner of English, whose language employs a pragmatic based discourse in contradistinction to a text-based discourse employed by English (Kim, 1989), begins to engage in verbal communication in English. The pragmatic-based discourse by the former language is defined as the discourse where communications rely largely on the information which is not expressed in language forms, but is recoverable from the context. On the contrary, the text-based discourse by the latter language is defined as the discourse where communications are based on the information that is clearly expressed in language forms. Kim rightfully argues that three concepts such as low/high context, semiotic proximity (personal distance), and final verb position contribute to making the differential bases for Korean and English discourse. Let us take up these three concepts and explain each in some detail, because doing so will help understand in part why Koreans learning English so often underuse discoursal information and the discourse in English sounds fragmented and is hard to fathom.

Kim's idea of the pragmatic-based discourse in Korean stems from his first concept of the 'high context' culture (Hall, 1976) where information is programmed with minimal detail in the transmitted message. Because of this, Koreans seldom correct you or explain things to you, and you are supposed to know what everybody knows. Since Koreans think that they are close to each other in terms of what they have experienced or can share, they are reluctant to jot down what has or does not have to be done. They expect more of others than they themselves offer to listeners. In a low context system, by contrast, most of the information is in the transmitted message in order to make up for what is missing in the context. Kim claims that this difference in information load affects the way Korean and English interweave the discourse. For example, the Korean discourse based on the high context culture tends to be less expressive because of the high degree of presupposed information. Kim notes:

> It is indeed perceived by the listener as an insult, a violation, or an intrusion into his personal space for the speaker/writer to provide detailed information beyond what is actually required. Therefore, those languages utilizing high context systems (mainly Asiatic languages such as Korean, Japanese, Chinese , etc.) may need to employ cohesive devices where mental capacities are pragmaticaly called for (p19).

On the other hand, the English discourse using a low context culture tends to be expressive because less information is assumed to be shared across ethnocultural boundaries. Thus, speakers of English at large need to provide detailed information as a common underlying bond for communication to be effective. In this sense, as Kim says, English utilizing the low context system may need to employ a set of cohesive devices where textual interweaving prevails. Other languages (mainly Indo-European languages) which utilize the low context system are French, German, etc.

The second concept Kim addresses in the theory of pragmatic flow of thought in Korean discourse is based on Koreans' interpersonal communication pattern. As many foreigners often witness, personal space for Koreans in an American sense is non existent and interpersonal touch is ever present. For this reason, Koreans seldom want to keep secret something they happen to have or know. To get rid of a certain privacy is even perceived as one typical way by which they can get closer to each other. Moreover, Koreans in general are notorious for even knowing the most intimate details about each other's personal affairs. Kim links this kind of Koreans' communicative behavior to their heavy reliance on non-verbal feedback and innuendos for each other's true feelings which a foreigner would invariably miss. That is why Koreans use their pragmatic world knowledge in the discourse itself to deduce the referent of the pronouns which are, in fact, suppressed on the surface.

The third concept for Kim's claim of the pragmatic-based discourse in Korean originates in the grammatical relationships within the sentence. In Korean sentence structures, the order of the various parts is determined not by grammatical function, as it is in English, but by the degree of importance. In other words, a sentence without the subject and/or the object is completely grammatical in so far as an indispensable verb comes at the end of it. Korean verbs which are functionally decisive entail various information such as honorifics, tense, mood, etc.. Thus, the verb has to stand in order to transmit the central message. Here are cited Kim's examples:

Speaker   *A: na.nun ecekkey chayk.ul hankwon sassta
                 (나-는 어저께 책-을 한-권 샀-다)
                 I TP yesterday book OM one volume bought
                 TP-Topic marker; OM-Object Marker
                 "I bought one volume of a book yesterday."

Speaker   *B: ediyse sassni? (어디서 샀니?)
                 "Where did (you) buy (it) ?"

As in the above discourse, the Korean discourse allows the subject *you(he, she, etc.)* and object *it* to be deleted without being ungrammatical. Kim conjectures that subject and object in this discourse structure are not required because speakers and hearers are assumed to fall back on an inherent mental capacity to make inferences beyond the amount of actual use of the language code appropriate to the given discourse. The three terms in the sentence *I* am asking *you* about *the book* that you bought yesterday would be missing in typical Korean discourse. Kim's reasoning about this permissable deletion is illuminating in that to spell out these grammatical elements may even cause a degree of stigmatization for the addressee, since every participant in the discourse is expected to abide by such suppression of pronouns in the communicative setting.

To recapitulate, Kim has made a claim that Korean discourse (i.e., pragmatic-based) differs from English discourse (i.e., text-based), the difference which he attributed to three concepts such as low/high context, personal space, and final verb position. As a result of this difference in discourse, native speakers of English find many difficulties in understanding what Koreans try to communicate in English, especially when they use personal pronouns in sentences. For the sake of simplicity, we will compare and contrast the second and third personal pronouns with a particular interest in determining

---

* The Yale Romanization system by Martin(1962) has been adopted for transliterating above Korean sentences and other words elsewhere throughout the chapter.

conditions for zero personal reference in subject/object positions in Korean discourse.

The second personal pronoun *you* in English diverges into more than five variants in Korean. One form 너 *"ne"* is prototypical for second person reference in Korean, equivalent to English *you*. The other forms (자네 *"chaney"* for the superior to the inferior, 당신 *"tangshin"* for spouse, 댁 *"tayk"* for the inferior to the superior, 선생 님 *"sonsaengnim"* for the respectful, etc.) are words which function as non-pronominal substitutes. The use of these forms is closely tied up with social relationships where participant-roles are lexicalized on the basis of the honorific system. That is, honorific expressions substitute for personal pronouns. To make the matter worse, the Korean language is said to maximize the efficiency of face-to-face communicative interaction in the 2nd personal pronominal system: once the speaker and the addressee show up on the communicative scene, there is no need to spell out the speaker as *I* and the addressee as *you*. This allows the Korean language to behave flexibly in suppressing some parts of the actual forms of lexemes in subject and object positions. To put it in a nutshell, spatiotemporal proximity (close personal space) of the participants by nature enables the intended message to be carried without maintaining the grammatical elements which express their roles. This verbal behavior by Koreans reflects "egocentricity" to use Lyon' s term, in that the speaker and the addressee, by virtue of being the speaker and the addressee respectively, cast themselves in the role of ego and relate everything to their own viewpoint. This observable egocentric behavior is liable to be carried-over into their communication in English, which perplexes English speakers trying to make a sense out of it.

The use of the third personal pronouns in the English discourse spoken by Koreans also presents a similar kind of problem—perhaps worse in this case—for foreigners. For example, English *he* diverges into more than three variants (i.e., 그 *"ku"*, 그이 *"kui"* for plain form, 그분 *"kupun"* for polite form, 형님 *"hyongnym"* for brother, 삼 촌 *"samchun"* for uncle, etc.) in Korean, and English *she* into more than four variants (i.e., 그녀 *"kunye"* for plain, 그분 *"kupun"* for polite, 누나 *"nuyna"* for elder sister, 숙모 *"sukmo"* for aunt, etc.). The variants in Korean are differentiated in their use according to the honorific system. In addition to these forms, it is interesting to note that with every lexicalized non-pronominal substitute it is possible to refer to a person outside the communicative situation. The general preference is to adopt lexicalized forms such as 형님 *"hyongnym"* for brother and 누님 *"nuynim"* for elder sister. The Korean equivalents for English third person reference are best described as quasiforms since the language does not possess third person pronouns comparable to the English ones. These quasiforms may not appear on the text because the Korean language pragmatically suppresses them, referred to as zero-expression in this section. This phenomenon is well explained in Kim's following pair of sentences:

Speaker A: Where is he ?
Speaker B: ϕ tutie kassta.(드디어 갔다)
at last went
"At last, (he) went."
(Speaker B interprets the question as that
Speaker A is asking about [John] who got
married a few minutes ago and he left on his
honeymoon.)

In (A), the nature of the question clearly indicates that the speaker realizes easily the identity of *he* by means of previously shared knowledge. By the same token, in (B), the deletion shows that the addressee realizes the identity of *he* by recourse to experiential knowledge. He is left to read out pragmatically what is missing in the ongoing discourse. Here again, the tendency to suppress information on the part of Koreans will deter their attempts to communicate with English speakers.

1.6. IDIOMATIC AND METAPHORICAL EXPRESSIONS

The native speaker of English uses more idiomatic expressions than he realizes. To the Korean speaker of English, one of the most irritating and frustrating aspects of the language is the formation of special expressions or idioms. The Korean speaker discovers, to his dismay, that there are hundreds of word combinations whose meaning bears little or no relationship to the individual words of which they are composed. He learns, for example, the words "call" and "off," and then some time later discovers that there is a special expression "call off" which means "cancel." What a hard time I had during my stay in the United States trying to understand such expressions as "talk through one's hat" (talk nonesense, e.g. Don't listen to him; he is talking through his hat.), "talk shop" (discuss business matters, e.g. Bob, stop talking shop. The ladies are waiting for us in the lounge.), "break up" (disturb, upset, e.g Nancy was broken up when she heard the news.), "(You had better) get your head together" (You'd better start thinking correctly.).

Americans early manifested the gift which they continue to show, the gift of the imaginative, slightly humorous phrase. To this gift belong such gems as "pull someone's leg" (tease or fool someone), "bark up the wrong tree" (attack the wrong thing), "face the music" (accept the consequences, however unpleasant), "fly off the handle" (become suddenly or violently angry or excited), "bury the hatchet" (stop fighting; make peace), "kick the bucket" (die), "the boys in the smoke-filled rooms" (the professional politicians who make their decisions independent of public opinion or good), "Starve a cold and feed a fever" (a successful operation (or action) can have unpleasant side-effects), and many more, alive with the national flavor. "I see the light at the end of the tunnel" (Victory is near at hand) was used several times during the Viet-Nam War situation by an American general, who became famous for his frequent use of the expression. Many such special expressions are unpredictable and patternless because they are derived from cultural factors other than language, from folklore, from famous proverbs, even from politics and current events. For those who are interested in expanding their repertoire on this line of expressions, there is one recent bilingual publication authored by Kim (1992) through Si-sa-yong-a-sa publishing company which listed some 160 curious expressions and proverbs of English with etymological details.

Idiomatic expressions are the heart of the English language and provide color, informality, charm and exactness in daily speech and writing. The expression, "breaking the ice" (promoting informality, e.g. His joke broke the ice and we all laughed) is very exact, and the expression, "cutting down" (She tried to cut down expenses after her husband's death) carries more power than the expression "reducing." These puzzling expressions have peculiar meanings and make little sense if translated literally.

A Korean doctor was told to "get on the ball" (to be alert; be efficient) while working in an American hospital. He immediately started translating this literally in his mind. It did not make sense to him until he consulted the dictionary after work. A literal transfer of the biblical idiom "heap coals of fire on his head" involves considerable distortion of meaning. A non-native speaker of English would consider that this is a reference to some new method for torturing enemies to death.

The fundamental trouble is that in transferring any content of the message, one should not be concerned with the precise words or units, but with the sets of components. In fact, one does not really transfer words but bundles of componential features. By transferring on the level of the surface structures, one is most likely to distort the message. In the transfer of idioms, there are usually complete redistributions of the componential structures. The meaning of the idiom, "heap coals of fire on his head" — its componential structure — must be completely redistributed, so that it can be carried over in a form such as "to be so good to one's opponent as to make him ashamed."

Some years ago I had a chance to get acquainted with one visiting Professor from an American university to the department of English of my university. One Saturday afternoon, we decided to hang out in Itaewon, one of the most exotic places to shop around in Seoul. Although our pockets were no less generous than what we wanted to splurge and I had a car to drive, he suggested that we try a Korean bus to get there. The moment we got on the bus, my American friend hailed to me and exclaimed, "Look, Dr. Park! That Korean pupil can pregnate a baby, can't he?" I retorted to him rather blatantly, "You're kidding, aren't you? I have never on earth heard such a bizzare story." When I turned around to him, I found him pointing to the name plate of one male student standing on the center isle of the bus, unmistakingly written "임신중" (literally in pregnancy). I answered that it is nothing but a name which cannot be imbued with any disgraceful meaning. He later confessed to me that it never crossed his mind that people can be named with such a strange combination of words. He went on further to comment that the student might have to have his name replaced in order to avoid being teased by his fellow students whereever he goes. Although ordinary Koreans would not embrace such a connotative association attached to that name, I surmised that a foreigner's spontaneous literal translation of it would be a natural instinct, no matter how odd that might sound like.

Some English idiomatic and metaphorical expressions can be redistributed and explained. There are approximate equivalents in Korean for some of the English metaphorical expressions which can be replaced by other figurative terms in Korean. The English expression "lay on the butter" can be redistributed in Korean in such a form as(비행기 태우다) "fly someone in a plane" or "take someone for a ride." It is interesting to note that there are many aphoristic usages in Korean with their English equivalents. Some examples of these are:

(행차 이후에 나팔)
After the march the trumpet sounds (or to lock the door after the horse is gone.).
(고통은 낙의 씨앗이다.)
Trouble is the seed of joy.
(정의는 필승이다.)
Righteousness will finally conquer.
(바늘 도둑이 소도둑 된다.)
He who steals a needle will become a cow thief.
(식자 우환이다.)
Much science (learning), much sorrow.
(동문서답)
Ask the east, answer from the west.
(큰 소리치는 사람은 실속이 없다.)
A barking dog is never a good hunter.
(세상에 비밀은 없다.)
Murder will out
(시장은 반찬이다.)
Hunger is the best sauce.
(끼리끼리 모인다.)
Birds of a feather flock together.
(밤 말은 쥐가 듣고 낮 말은 새가 듣는다.)
Walls have ears.
(신분에 맞게 살아라.)

Cut your coat according to your cloth.
(날개돋힌 듯이 팔린다.)
It sells like hotcakes.
(개천에서 용났다.)
A black hen laid white eggs.
(시작이 반이다.)
To begin is half the job.
(장부일언 중천금)
A word of honor is as good as a bond.
(호랑이에게 물려가도 정신만 차리면 살 수 있다.)
Though chased by a tiger, if one gathers his wits, he may live.
(우이 독경)
Casting pearls before swine.

Paul S. Crane(1967: 196) says that these familiar epigrams help to point up the obvious fact that the same ideals and pearls of wisdom are found in both Eastern and Western literature and in their heritages. He concludes his chapter, saying that there is an awareness of God, tolerance of human frailty, recognition of moral virtue, and an image of the ideal man.

MOG—YOK—TANG

1.7.   EMOTIVE MEANINGS

We have seen so far how inter-lingual difficulties between two cultures result, because surface forms of two languages do not section semantic concepts in a uniform way. Since certain cultural features have few, if any, one to one correspondence between two languages because of intrinsic differences in the cultural background of each language, it is inevitable that inter-cultural opacity (cf. Song 1915: 54) also results. A person either exposed to Korean culture or to American culture is confronted with cultural opacities at all levels—within a phrase, within a sentence and even down to individual words.

It is interesting to note that certain expressions refer to the same objects but their associations are considerably different. The association a Korean word "mog-yok-tang" stirs in the Korean mind is quite different from the association its English equivalent "bathhouse" gives. Some Korean words are easily translatable but do not conjure up the proper image in English. "Tojang" can be called "seal" or "stamp" in English but the association is not exactly the same. "Toshirak" is not exactly what the English speaker means by a lunchbox or "Yakbang" is not what he means when he says "drugstore." The word "kohyang" evokes a complex of favorable emotional reactions to Korean people in such a way that none of its English equivalents like "hometown" or "native place" can ever match. Even with the most sensitive "feel" of the Korean speaker toward an emotive item of English, it is a tantalizing task to match the emotive meaning in English (Song 1975: 52).

Barbara R. Mintz says in her column for The Korea Times that whenever she thinks of a "haksaeng," immediately the picture of a middle-school boy complete with black uniform, cap, and grey school bag pops into her mind. She goes on to say that a "sajang" to her has to be potbellied, pompous, and rich, and he is not just the president of a company, but is the idea of what the president of a company must look like.

It is perfectly understandable that English speakers living in Korea should have to use in their speech things, events and beings that are wholly unique to Korean culture. Some words they frequently incorporate into their speech are: "anju" (안주), "ondol" (온돌), "yo" (요), "punshik" (분식), "yontan" (연탄), "mandu" (만두), "yogwan" (여관), "kibun" (기분), "mot" (멋), "yamche" (얌체), etc. Professor Song explains the word "mot" in his translation of Professor C. D. Pi's essay entitled "mot" in the Korea Journal (April, 1971): The Korean word "mot" has a broad range of meanings from stylishness, elegance, gracefulness, smartness, dandyism, attractiveness, tastefulness, being well-groomed, being soigne, charm, zest or whim. Barbara R. Mintz describes "yamche" in her column for The Korea Times: it is a little hard to say exactly what a yamche is, but I certainly know one when I see one—like the guy who stole my taxi right out from under me today. What a yamche! It is extremely doubtful that one is able to carry over the Korean "flavor, spirit, and zeitgeist" (Carroll 1955: 226) inherent in these words to another culture with an acceptable degree of fidelity. These kinds of words peculiar to Korean culture are either untranslatable or if it is possible to translate them, it is awkward or misleading to do so.

One telltale episode which I was recently told by Professor Kim (one of my former students now teaching at an American university and currently visiting Seoul) is the story of one Korean doctor who started a job at a local hospital in the suburban area of an exclusively white neighborhood in Chicago. He told me the following story which resulted from the Americans' apparently misled translation of a Korean last name. In one fall semester, his class was inundated with an unusually large number of Asian–American students. When he, as usual, browsed through the names of students on the class roster to get to know invidivual names, his eyes caught up with the last name of one student, Dwight Kwa. Although he originally thought he might be of South Asian descent by face and English accents, a lurking curiosity led him to ask what nationality he was. Dwight told Professor Kim the full fledged story of why his Korean family had to switch their original last name Quack(곽) to Kwa(과) — the last name which they were forced to newly adopt with much regret:

"My family immigrated to the USA in 1976 when I was ten years old because my father, a medical doctor at a major hospital in Seoul, was disgruntled with social turmoil and the nation's political instability at that time. Three years after he studied at an American medical school he passed the Licensure examinations administered by the board of American Medical Doctors. After many years as an intern and resident, he finally succeeded in finding the position of attending physician at a local hospital. After some days of orientation for new doctors, the hospital administration invited him and other fellow doctors to a wine and cheese party for social gathering. At the party, every body was supposed to bear a name tag, written "Hello, my name is____. "Ignorant of any cultural loopholes in all his honesty, my father attached his name card, written in "Hello, my name is Dr.

Quack (pronounced as /kwak/.)" As soon as he showed himself on the floor of the lounge, everybody around burst into a laughter. My father heard someone even jokingly asking,"Here comes Dr. Quack! How come you could be a care-taking doctor for patients. Your name even tells us you are a fraudulant pretender to medical skill(돌팔이 의사 in its Korean translation)." Of course, this was a prankish joke typical of Americans who make it a rule to entertain by exchanging harmless jokes among colleagues. Nonetheless, my father got a bit serious because he believed that he was being ridiculed in public. On the next day, he obtained a court order which allowed our family name to be switched to "Kwa", which sounds closest to the Korean original. Since then, we had to use the last name "Kwa," but not "Quack."

The case of Mr. Kwa's family clearly exemplifies how the emotive meaning of a certain word or words affects people of different culture.

As illustrated above, Korean and English have so distinctly different structures that one can not hope to reproduce the structure of the original Korean in English, using the same number of words and sentences and always expressing the same Korean word by the same English word. A Korean sentence or paragraph may become shorter or longer when put into English depending on the structures involved. Certain cultural features have no direct equivalents because of intrinsic differences in the cultural background of each language. In any transfer there is an inevitable modification in the meaning and consequently some degree of distortion and loss.

In the process of cross-cultural communication, especially in the case of Korean and English having quite different grammatical and semantic structures, the speaker of either language, instead of going directly from one set of surface structures to another, actually goes through a seemingly roundabout process of grammatical analysis, transfer, and restructuring. That is to say, the speaker first analyzes the message of what he is going to say into its simplest and structurally clearest forms, transfers it at this level, and then restructures it to the level in the target language which is most appropriate for the person with whom he intends to communicate. This process happens simultaneously in a twinkling of an eye in the speaker's mind. His brain functions "by an intra-subjective communing of a split personality," as Quine (1964: 475) put it. One prime candidate which fits into this roundabout process (Kim,1989) is English and Korean complex sentences consisting of multiple embedding. Let's take, for example, the English sentence "Chulsoo keeps a cat —." This sentence can get expanded by adding conceptual chunks to the right of the BASE sentence: Chulsoo keeps a cat [that killed a rat [that ate bread [that was rotten]]]. On the other hand, the counterpart sentence in Korean expands the sentence by stacking conceptual chunks to the left of the BASE: [[[철수가 기르는]고양이가 죽였던]쥐가 먹었던]빵은 썩었다. In other words, English sentences of such structure are translated into Korean in an exactly opposite constituent order. Also notice that the Korean translation unwantedly shifts their focus *cat* to *bread*. Because of this structural asymmetry, direct translation is not always possible and, thus, alternative functional translations are often taken in reality. It is needless to say that great difficulties are experienced in processing Korean sentences into English equivalents, or English into Korean because of these opposite branching directions.

Eugene A Nida (1969: 484) compares this roundabout procedure to the experience of the hiker who finds that a stream he must cross is so deep and the current so swift that he cannot risk crossing over directly from one point to another. Therefore, he goes downstream to a ford, at which point the transfer from one side to another can be made with the least possible danger to himself and his equipment. He can then go back upstream to the point which best suits him. The processes of analysis are, however, not so easy as they might seem, for they undergo at least three different baffling stages: the grammatical relationships between constituent parts, the referential meanings of the semantic units, and the connotative values of the grammatical structure and the semantic units.

Chapter 2

CROSS-CULTURAL PROBLEMS

One might argue that cross-cultural communication is, in the absolute sense, impossible. It is very tempting to take such a position from time to time especially in carrying over what is culturally original in one country to another. We recognize the incommensurability of languages. Absolute communication is, however, impossible not only between languages but also within a language. Eugene A. Nida (1959: 483) remarks that effective interlingual communication is always possible, despite seemingly enormous differences in linguistic structures and cultural features. The relative adequacy of interlingual communication is based on two fundamental factors: semantic similarities between languages, due in large measure to the common core of human experience, and fundamental similarities in the syntactic structures of languages, especially at the so-called kernel or core level.

My experiences demonstrate that a successful cross-cultural communication can never be accomplished without understanding thoroughly the socio-cultural and emotional backgrounds of the target languages. Even if you have a thorough grasp of their socio-cultural backgrounds, still there must be some degree of distortion and loss in the process of transfer. In cross-cultural communication where distinctions depend much more on perceptual differences than on conceptual classifications, divergences between languages are not too great. When, however, one touches upon the subtle areas of the original culture of the target language, where distinctions depend primarily on conceptual classifications, the differences between languages are much greater. It must be pointed out also that patterns of emotive meaning tend to show even greater discrepancies than distinctions based on conceptualization. Speaking more specifically, the more convincing the dialogue of the Korean original, the more difficult it will be to express it into convincing English dialogue (Rutt 1966: 141-64).

Truly language erects as many barriers as bridges. Cultural barriers with all cultural overtones and implications are much more difficult to overcome than linguistic barriers, although it is always hard to draw a sharp line between linguistic and cultural elements. They are so closely intermingled that they are usually inseparable in most cases. There is an intimate and inevitable relationship between the language structure of a culture and the modes in which the people think and act. Also language is the ordinary and most distinctively human way in which people communicate their concepts and state their judgments. People of any culture can think only the thoughts their language permits them to think, and their language in turn helps them construct their universe. The Korean language, for example, uses different words for counting depending on what is being counted—people (한분, 두분 or 한놈, 두놈), birds (한마리, 두마리 or 한수, 두수), fish (한마리, 두마리), and so forth. It also makes many more distinctions in levels of speech, according to age, social status, and degree of intimacy, than do the Indo-European languages.

When languages like Korean and English are remote from each other not only in linguistic structure but also in cultural background, heart-to-heart communication in the true sense of the word is extremely difficult to effect. Thought and speech are not two different things which are casually connected, like a motorcar and its driver. They are closely linked together like cause and effect, like form and substance, so that a thought expressed in two different ways is practically two different thoughts. Furthermore, a mere grasp of linguistic units such as the pronunciation, vocabulary and grammar of the language concerned and a thorough understanding of the sociocultural and emotional background of the users of the languages are two completely different things. The greater the language difference, the greater the cultural distance.

In addition to the linguistic difficulties which have to be overcome, an intruder into another culture has to tackle the greater difficulties arising from the different socio-cultural backgrounds. Cross-cultural communication is a cultural as well as linguistic performance based on an underlying bilingual competence. As Edward T. Hall aptly puts it in *The Silent Language*, communication is culture, and culture is communication (Hall 1959: 93). This is another way of saying that the very way we organize our lives is part of a network of communication and that those who would function within a society or culture other than their own must learn its cultural as well as its linguistic code. Misunderstanding and cultural shock result largely from the different modes of thought and cultural patterns between the two countries rather than from the linguistic incompetence of the user of the language. A person exposed to foreign culture is confronted with cultural pitfalls at all points in both verbal and nonverbal communication.

So far the main concern of linguistics has been with grammaticalness which belongs to the study of competence (knowledge of the rules for understanding and producing grammatical sentences) in a Chomskyan sense, and acceptability which belongs to the study of performance (the actual use of language in concrete situations) has been a side issue in the agenda of generative grammar which gives off heat. The workable ability we need in actual social contexts, however, consists not only of Chomskyan competence, but also of knowledge of appropriate situated language use, e.g. social rules of language use. Not only grammaticality (competence) but also performance (social acceptability of utterances) should be stressed. This extended notion of linguistic competence might be termed as "communicative competence."

Separating language from the cultural and social contexts can hardly be conceivable. The meaning of utterances is socially defined and depends on the social contexts in which the utterances are used. For example, the Korean language makes abundant use of honorific forms pivotal to the characteristics of the Korean culture. The society where Confucianism prevails always tends to calibrate its people on the scale of an asymmetrical relationship (i.e., vertical but not horizontal), the relationship of which is transformed into expressions of honorific forms. Thus, levels of speech are determined, depending upon *who* is addressing *whom* under *what* relationship. This asymmetrical participant relationship the Korean language utilizes indeed seems disparaging for foreigners whose language is based on mutual equality in social status. Moreover, the mastery of the honorific system of the Korean language becomes a major task they are confronted with. The social meaning which an utterance can have in a social context is extremely important in cross-cultural communication. Referentially equivalent linguistic forms in Korean and English might have different connotative values or social meanings. The word "fat" may have positive and complimentary connotation in Korean culture, whereas it may have negative and derogatory connotation in American culture. In contrast, the word "public bath house (목욕탕 in Korean)" has obscene connotations for many Americans who think that this facility is frequented only by deviates, whereas for Koreans it is a common household term for a place where any one can take a bath at one's convenience.

Culture includes all the material and nonmaterial aspects of a way of life which are shared and transmitted among members of a society. All this is learned behavior. From the early years of childhood many of the patterns of later life begin to be established. As one grows older he learns anew and modifies habits, values, beliefs, concepts, etc, but, until one gets into touch with another culture, these intangible elements function subconsciously within one's inner self. Apart from material things such as food, clothing, housing, vehicles, etc., the non-material elements form so much a part of one's life that one is scarcely aware of them unless one is actually exposed to a different culture.

Different social institutions like school, church, hospital, reformatory, etc., present baffling problems to cross-cultural communication especially between the persons of developed countries and those of developing countries. There are some social institutions and some peculiar names or items attached to them in one culture which another culture does not possess. Language is so culture-sensitive that some words are not so frequently used in one culture as they are in another culture. The word "cafeteria", one of the most frequently used words in the U.S.A. is seldom used in Korea. To those who are not accustomed to sitting on a toilet, the Western style of commode is very uncomfortable.

Throughout this chapter, I will highlight not only the cultural ramifications typical of Koreans, but also exemplify the cultural shocks I experienced verbally or non-verbally during my first year of stay in the United States of America. Unfortunately, I have no hard facts, figures or research findings at my fingertips, so all I can offer you are my own intuitive feelings and reflections on the subject. The large part of what I am going to describe may also be true of those countries belonging to the sphere of influence of Confucianism and Buddhism.

The cross-cultural difference between Americans and Koreans, in a large sense, can be interpreted as the differences between Occidental and Oriental peoples. More detailed observation, however, may reveal that each act and event smacks of native touch of each country, a distinction which is visible to the sensitive observer as peculiarly Korean, rather than Japanese or Chinese, and Americans, rather than English or Canadian.

2.1. PUZZLING U.S. MORES

The Dutch Treat

A few weeks after I began to study in the new environment of graduate school of the University of Hawaii, I was introduced to an American high-school teacher from New York City. As an East–West Center grantee, he had been studying Japanese and Chinese for one year. There being something common between us (we had been high school teachers a short time before and were now students again), soon we became very intimate. One day he suggested we go to a Korean restaurant, saying that he knew a place not far from school where they served a wonderful Korean food, kalbi (barbecued beef ribs). I went wild over the prospect of eating Korean kalbi.

That afternoon at the Korean restaurant, we ordered kalbi and a bowl of rice with kimchi for each of us. I had longed for Korean food for so long that I enjoyed it very much for the first time since coming to Hawaii. After eating all the food which was achingly delicious for me, we headed for the cashier, my friend going before me. He paid and went out. I was going out, assuming that my friend had already paid for me. But the girl said, "Three dollars and fifty cents please." At that moment I blushed and felt keenly what "going Dutch" in American means, although I had heard about it many times before I came to America.

In Korea, the one who first suggests going out for dinner or drinks, pays not only for his own but also for his friend or whoever reaches the cashier first also pays for his friend. Korea's admirable tradition is that people battle over the bill and sometimes even engage in combat over the honor. The pride that someone evinces in winning the struggle is a welcome contrast to the feeling that a person experiences when he is stuck with the bill in America. The American custom of paying separately is really disturbing to a Korean who has not experienced it. There is something cold and solitary that insinuates itself in this habit that is unsettling to the soul.

Of course, once you get used to it, you may feel that it is a more rational and convenient custom. Yet the Korean way at least makes paying or not paying for your dinner as much fun as the dinner itself. As a word of advice, Americans, having read this section, do not necessarily have to stick to the Korean tradition of paying the bill for the party of people. It is because this old tradition seems to fade out slowly among the young generation who are keenly aware of the facets of the American culture and also understand the bright side of "going Dutch." When thrown into a position where such a decision is being called for, it might be a better idea to wait and see what group of people you are dealing with and how they are likely to act. In such a case when you are meeting friends or even businessmen who you know are educated in America, you are more than welcome to pay your own bill, unless otherwise informed.

Gifts

A few days before Christmas, I was invited to an American family home in Honolulu with some East-West Center grantees. Each of us was introduced to other American guests. There lay a heap of gifts each of the guests had brought for his (or her) hostess. To my great surprise, the hostess, in the middle of the party, suddenly picked up the gifts one by one and showed them to everybody. I was most embarrassed and ashamed when my small gift to the hostess was opened and picked up for everybody to see. In Korea, gifts should not be opened in the presence of the donor. Gifts are supposed to be opened in private.

Dr. Kleinjans, the president of the East-West Center, came to Seoul last spring. The East-West Center Alumni Association in Korea held a reception in his honor. In the latter part of the reception, a small gift of a gold ring was presented to him. He opened the box and showed the ring to everybody to show immediate appreciation. A Korean hotel girl serving us beverages seemed to be shocked at the sight.

Here it might be interesting to compare Koreans' subsumed character underlying gift-opening to Americans' conspicuous and rather hilarious behavior. Koreans usually do not open the gift in front of the presenter for two reasons I can stipulate. One reason has to do with Korean people's admiration of maturity which denies showing emotion to others at first sight. At the heart of the Korean culture lies a moral lesson that it is childish for an adult to pick up the gift and open it up right away for bragging, when presented. Some people even like to draw an analogy between that breed of adult and a child who licks over a candy without much awareness, right after it is being given to him. I believe that the delayed gift-opening by Koreans reveals one aspect of the Korean culture which cherishes the moral value of being vicarious and indirect, and dictates hiding their emotion up front and releasing it in due course.

Another reason underlies the receiver's graceful intention to save the presenter from running into possibly unexpected embarassment, when the gift is being opened in public. There are two possibilities which one may run into when the receiver decides to open the gift in front. On the one hand, when the gift happens to be well suited to the receiver's taste in size, color, and what not, the giver may turn out to be an instantaneous hero or heroine which deserves deep appreciation. This is in deed a good scenario. On the other hand, in all probability the worst scenario is equally possible. That is, when the gift turns out to be unsuitable to the receiver's taste for any imaginable reasons possible and also this is somehow being made public (or insinuated), the feeling of embarassment (as I myself experienced) or perhaps shame will be nothing but a remorseful feeling that may swirl through the giver's blood stream. Characteristic of Korean culture is the safeguard of avoiding this possible default situation with which the giver may be confronted.

Bargaining

Price haggling is a very common phenomenon which every one takes for granted when Koreans shop at markets. This habit seems so deeply ingrained in the minds of native Koreans that it often consciously or unconsciously affects their strategy in shopping. When I first went shopping, I thought it was possible to bargain in America as I do in Seoul. The shop woman thought at first that I had misunderstood her, but when she realized what I was driving at she stiffened visibly like a woman of honor to whom one has made a shady proposal. She gave me to understand, politely but plainly, that her prices could not be reduced. Her resolute bearing was so unmistakable that only a fool would have persisted.

An exception, though, could be the car dealers in America, especially used-car dealers, with whom one has to go through the ordeal of a see-saw type bargaining. Naturally, a language barrier would clearly be a disadvantage for non-native speakers of English. But one can suggest the same word of advice for foreigners shopping at

Korean markets. Some foreigners who are not fully immersed in Korean culture tend to make a sweeping generalization that they can adopt such a bargain strategy at every Korean store, even including Department stores (백화점). Although the habit of price haggling persisted throughout the old times of Korea, for a contemporary era we rather witness the gradually firm establishment of pricing at most major Korean markets, let alone Department stores. In reality, reduction of the price appears to depend on various amorphous factors such as a saleperson's generosity, the quality of the merchandise, the net margin, the place and time where such a transaction takes place, etc. Thus, it is advisable for foreigners to try haggling over the price only if the situation convinces them that it is permissable on all accounts.

Home Invitations

At the end of my first summer session, I was invited to an American family home by one of my classmates. He said there was going to be a party at his home and some of his friends would come. I was really curious about the first American home party I was going to attend. I went without eating supper, thinking that food would be served as in a Korean home party. But there was only light food, such as peanuts, popcorn, crackers and some cheese which were served for drinking but not for satiating my hunger.

I do not mean to generalize too much about American home parties since they are all likely to be different. The first party I went to in America, I presume, was one only for drinking. But there is a clear distinction between American and Korean parties in general. In Korean society, an invitation to someone's house in the evening normally means an invitation to dinner. In American society, such an invitation often means a nice chat over a cup of coffee and possibly some ice cream and cake unless otherwise informed. Korean students, when they receive such an invitation for the first time through an international hospitality program, come back to their empty apartment hungry and exhausted. When I left his house, every restaurant was closed, and so I had to go to bed without supper that night.

In a similar Korean situation, you would be served not only with enough drink but also with abundant food. You would be asked earnestly either by your friend or by his or her mother to go on eating and drinking more and more, almost to the extreme of making themselves nuisances.

No matter how humble the home, there is a warm welcome and refreshment for the visitor who enters the gate. A Korean host or hostess seems to have your best interests too much at heart. At times his or her excessive kindness merely fails to take your wants and desires into consideration, so that you might be put to inconvenience. This is a manifestation of excessive kindness which is motivated entirely by good intentions.

A Korean host (or hostess) will thank you for honoring his home by your presence, and giving your time to share his poor fare. He will usually remark, "We have nothing to offer you, but will you please eat heartily?"

Your joining helps a Korean family suddenly come to life. A natural bridge is made when you start talking and breaking the ice in the family divided by age and sex. In Korea, you are given the privilege of visiting a friend's home under any circumstances without any special festive occasion. I recall that when I was a boy, the small room was always noisily filled with my father's friends for no particular reason. In rural villages there is still a custom that is called "village visiting" in which you go to your friends' home in the evening (usually after supper) as if you had an appointment.

In an American home, however, nothing is more distressing than to have a guest entering your family abode without making an appointment in advance. (Even formal invitations are usually made in Korea a day or two ahead or the same day so that the invitation may not sound ostentatious, whereas in the United States invitations are usually made far in advance, sometimes a week or two ahead.)

The following is one unhappy episode in point which a friend of mine living in the USA revealed to me, the story of which is reminiscent of a cultural clash between him (living in New England, the Northeastern part of the USA) and his Korean visitor from New York who was apparently not acculturated to American culture with a couple of years of living in the USA. One Saturday evening, my friend, a Korean professor, and his family were having an outdoor barbeque party with one couple coming over from New York. The joy of the party was about to culminate, when Korean short ribs were sizzling on the grill with a chain of rising smoke and a cadre of children flew a frizbee on the well groomed lawn of the backyard.

Every body was indulged in digging into delicious food, sitting over the bench of the patio. All of a sudden, a phone inside rang. When Professor Kim got to the phone, he discovered that he was having another visitor, Mr. Lee, from New York, who was his senior by ten years (10년선배) at a Korean university. Mr. Lee told Professor Kim that his family of three and his parents-in-law (visiting from Korea) were out to tour around in town for the day and would like to come over to his house for a chat. Professor Kim explained to him the situation that he was having one couple already visiting and they would stay over the night, and added that he wouldn't mind their joining the barbeque party in progress. About an half hour later, Mr. Lee and his party arrived with a box of juicy Korean pears and walked over through the side door to the backyard. After heartily welcoming them, Professor Kim introduced them to his friendly couple, and the party went along very smoothly to the point where no one was conscious of how late the party was when it was over. Around 11 P.M. after every body cleaned up the table and the patio, Professor Kim expected the Lee famliy to leave, because he naturally thought that at that late night they must have made hotel reservations for a night stay. However, he came to know that Mrs. Lee told his wife that they did not make reservations and they sort of entertained the idea of staying over the night in his house. Since Professor Kim's house had only three bedrooms (which would be taken by his family of three and the guest of three) and a room for his study, it was impossible to accomodate them (all five people with his little daughter) in any spare room that he did not have. Professor Kim, so much americanized in thought and behavior, did not appreciate Mr. Lee's unwanted visit to his home with his own guests and, moreover, his intention to try out his hospitality by asking an additional room of him. As a matter of fact, Professor Kim and his wife could have squeezed the situation out and permitted themselves to let them sleep on the floor of the living room or his study. But all that did matter to them at that time was that they wanted to teach Mr. Lee and his wife a lesson that an unwanted visit to the American home cannot be welcome and it was their sole responsibility to provide lodging for themselves and especially for their own guests, given the situation that they never asked for it beforehand. Consequently, they were made out to reluctantly leave and had to look for a hotel to stay at. At a later point, Professor Kim's wife told him that she got the news that Mr. Lee and his wife were severely chastised by his parents-in-law for his unpreparedness, not to mention the couple themselves launched into a big family feud along the way when they looked for a motel at that late hour. After that incident, Professor Kim told me that the Lee family neither phoned them nor visited their home. (Now Professor Kim regrets that he did not extend his welcoming hands to the Lee family, although he does not think that forcing the host to accomodate the guests with no permit in advance is a civilized cultural practice.)

You should not take Koreans' saying "no" at face value, especially at the dinner table or when you offer him gifts. Koreans usually decline your offer to take more just out of courtesy. Usually your Korean guest refuses, expecting to be asked again. Common courtesy demands that you urge your Korean guest to take more several times. Even if you think you are making yourself a nuisance to your guest by urging, it is safer and better to insist. I remember many times that at their first suggestion I refused out of courtesy, but they never asked me again to my disappointment.

The same is true in the case of the offering of gifts. When you bring gifts to your Korean friends, they will say, "Oh, you shouldn't" or "Take it back with you." If they accept the gifts immediately without refusing at least once or twice, they will be considered people of no face (chemyen epnun saram) (Kim 1975: 13). It will take time for you to understand the undertones of the Korean way of refusal.

I once heard a Peace Corps volunteer talk about her first experience at her Korean friend's home, which well summarizes the characteristics of a Korean mother's excessive kindness. Donna was excited as she had before her a large table overflowing with various kinds of food and soft drinks. She loved food and tried everything on the table. Her Korean friend's old mother had watched her like a hawk and kept urging her to eat more or to try one dish or another.

The mother was so persistent that Donna became annoyed. She thought it was obvious that she liked the food as she ate some of everything and had said several times that it was delicious. The mother continued to egg her on, and, finally, picked up a raw oyster, reached across the table, and put it in her rice bowl. She was so surprised that she stopped eating abruptly. The mother then asked what was wrong. Donna didn't say anything, but felt like replying that she knew how to feed herself.

One day a woman Peace Corps volunteer newly assigned to my university came to my office and told me about her first surprising experience when she moved in with a Korean family and started eating her first dinner with them. The old Korean mother not only kept urging Nancy to eat more but also ran her fingers over Nancy's body from her hair to her shoulders and back, so that Nancy was extremely embarrassed. She was very much afraid that the old mother might have had some prurient interest in her.

The old mother, however, had no intention whatever of putting Nancy in an awkward position, nor did she have any lewd thoughts about her. A Korean person often expresses his or her affection for children or young people by smoothing down their heads or shoulders. The mother may have thought of Nancy as a daughter.

2.2. DRINKING MANNERS

One Saturday afternoon I was drinking in an American drinking establishment with some of my new American friends. What surprised me at that moment was that whenever the bar girl brought some bottles of beer, she made change and took away a certain amount out of the money in front of each drinker. It was only I who did not put money on the table (We Korean people pay the total amount for drinks when we leave.). When the money placed in front of each person ran out, the girl proceeded to take another person's money. What was still more surprising to me was that each one filled his own glass and drank without passing the glass to his friend and without asking him to drink. I was somewhat bewildered because I had never poured my own glass before. They went on drinking and drinking without eating any snacks or side dishes as we do in Korea. I drank only a few glasses of beer partly because it was somewhat awkward for me to fill my own glass and partly because I did not want to drown my empty stomach in beer. I sat with them for quite a while, but I went out as sober as ever. Walking all the way to the school dormitory, I realized that there was something seemingly cold and unfriendly in the American way of drinking.

There are some rules in the Korean way of drinking. One is that you never drink without something to eat. Drink is always served with food or suitable side dishes. Even if it is only Kimchi, you always have something to eat, usually three or four different dishes. Another is that you never fill your own glass, but always pour for someone else. When you finish a glass (or a bowl as the case may be) you pass it to another person and fill it for him. This shows friendship and respect. When you receive a glass, you hold it with your right hand, and support it with your left, while your respectful friend pours. Then you drink and give it back and pour using your right hand, supporting it with your left. With intimate friends you can forget the two-hand routine. If girls are present, they do the pouring. It is permissible to give a glass to a winehouse girl and is even recommended. To the contrary, Americans are conspicuous in maintaining a somewhat self-centered drinking manner. No doubt it is unthinkable (or even barbarous) for Americans to hand over the glass or cup one emptied to the next person. Some informal statistics rather recently released by the Catholic church in the USA epitomizes Americans' sensitivity toward a sanitary drinking style, which was heightened by an AIDS epidemic syndrome. In an early stage of research on this uncurable disease when the National Health Institute reported through the media that an AIDS virus can be carried by bodily fluids emitting from human contact such as kissing, uncleaned utensils after use (i.e., cups, spoons, chopsticks, etc.), etc., most congregation was afraid of drinking holy wine in the Mass at the church in fear of catching a contagious virus through the repeatedly used cup. As an aftermath, it was reported that American priests experienced much agony in having to drink up all remaining holy wine they prepared for the congregation.

Using only one hand in offering a glass or handing something to one's respected elders is considered very rude. How many times I felt I was being ill-treated when an American friend poured a glass for me with one hand or he received my glass with one hand. At the old meetings of North Koreans and Americans at the Demilitarized Zone, the North Koreans insulted Americans many times by handing them glasses or other things with one hand only. I wonder whether Americans realized they were being insulted (cf. Kim 1975: 14).

Although the rule is not always true, you will seldom start tippling in Korea before noon and usually not until about 5:00 or 6:00. Plans are occasionally made, but usually are of a spur-of-the-moment nature started with some innocent question like "Are you free tonight?" An American Peace Corps volunteer comments on drinking in Korea this way:

> Drinking is the Korean national sport and the training table is always set. Since the season has not been established yet and no one has been foolish enough to challenge the Republic of Korea for the title, training is year round and seven days a week. You either drink with women or you drink without them. Usually you will do the latter first until some fool says. "Hey, let's go where they have some woman." I say "fool" because he who suggests, pays.

Amidst all the passing and receiving, there is usually amiable talking and singing. When you drink in a beerhall or in a cabaret (both Korean and Western style drinking) you go up and sing with the band. When someone is singing, one beats on the table with a spoon or chopsticks; if one is not the singer, then one should make appropriate noises and comments. When you drink with women at a Korean-style drinking place, they take turns singing for you.

Another rule is that you should not refuse a glass offered by your friend unless you have a convincing reason to do so. It is an insult to refuse a glass. Very few Koreans, once they've been drinking, are understanding when you say you have had enough (There is always a fellow who pushes someone else to keep on drinking even if he does not really want to.). This is a constant sore point when Americans living in Korea drink with their Korean friends, until they discover that, if one has had enough, one accepts another glass with thanks and then either throws it out or pours it back in the pot when the other person is not looking. At times this is a good thing to know if you want to maintain good personal relations and a sound stomach.

I still remember the drinking party held in honor of the new Peace Corps volunteer assigned to the high school where I once taught. In accordance with Korean drinking tradition the principal passed the young American teacher his empty cup and then filled it with sake (Cheong-Jong) for him. At this point the new teacher did not seem to have the faintest inkling what custom dictated he should do. Without drinking the cup filled by the principal, he gave him back the same glass still completely full. This caused everyone at the table to dissolve into puddles of tears from uncontrollable laughter. He was fatally bewildered by it all and told me a few months later that drinking, its forms and feelings, became somewhat of a preoccupation with him, or at least a serious avocation.

Although it is a rather recent event, modern technology put into full stride Koreans' entertainment of combining drinking and singing at the so-called "Singing Room (노래방)." With the advent of the Karaoke machinery, many Koreans are exulted to sing with a microphone, following through the lines of the song shown on the huge screen, while they listen to the melodies flowing from the amplifier. Since this method of singing draws on people's potential to sing, even without knowing the exact lines of unpopular songs and their melodies, they succeeded in bringing Karaokae culture to center stage. And any one who is or wants to be immune to this singing culture may not be welcome by the members of the group he needs to get associated with. Since it is my understanding that foreigners in general feel reluctant to sing in public for no particular reason, the culture of "Karaokae" appears to pose some nuisance for them, unless they are fond of singing.

To capitalize on Koreans' preponderance to sing loudly, while drinking, I here share one nonchalant story which put into serious trouble a group of Korean-Americans living in Warwick, Rhode Island. One sunny Saturday night, the Chang family, along with a band of their helpers at a local Korean church in Boston, moved their household stuffs into their newly built house. Having finished moving things, the Chang couple threw a party for them in return for their all help. After supper, they cheered themselves up by drinking beer and wine, and the party got bit more boisterous than they originally planned. When they got their face flushed up with over indulgence of alcohol, they began to sing Korean songs in chorus to the point of yelling, tapping on the food table with silver chopsticks or even with spoons, as they often did in Korean homes in Seoul. The ecstasy of the party was abruptly interruppted with deadly silence, when a pair of iron clad police men knocked on the front door of the house. They first apologized for their breaking into their party, but then explained to innocent looking Koreans that their check point was prompted by someone in the neighborhood who reported to the Station that some kind of verbal fighting seemed to be going on in their house. Mr. Chang and his friends could not understand the accusation and told the policemen that all they did was to sing Korean songs that probably sounded like meaningless cacaphony to their caucasian neighbors. But they argued that singing songs loudly cannot be equal to verbal argument. Nonetheless, the policemen insisted that the party should be stopped immediately and handed over Mr. Chang a warning ticket for violating the civil code of domestic violence set by the town counsel. Also the policemen read the code restrictions to Mr. Chang and others that if the party was going to be boisterous like this one, it should then be held in a public place, but not in a residential neighborhood. Although they did not want to be overruled by these unpopular civil regulations at least in their back boned Korean minds, they had no choice but to bring the party to an end, so as to quell the matter surreptitiously.

In many respects the ways and whys of American tippling illuminate a great number of the social and cultural difference between the two countries. After a long day of toil and stress one of the most relaxing and warming experiences in Korea is to drop into one's favorite place to drink with friends. It is there that you can shuck off the formality that seems to inject so much tension into Korean social relationships, and then relax, confide and joke with your friends. The exchange of cups, uninhibited talk, laughter or singing would be much harder to find in an American drinking place. During my stay in America, I observed much more solitary drinking and more reserve in behavior. At an American bar you see solitary drinkers sipping their beverage on a stool without talking to the person next to them. In contrast, you will more often than not see a group of people drinking over a line of shared dishes at any Korean bar or restaurant.

2.3. FAMILY LIFE AND WOMEN STATUS

The American way of social contract prevails in every walk of life. When the marriage contract between a husband and wife dissolves, the American wife goes back to "miss" status. It is still difficult for the Korean people, like Japanese and Chinese who have been influenced by Confucianism for the past thousand years, to understand how a woman who once had marital status, can regain her original state of virginity, "Miss." When I first came to America, I was surprised to find that there are so many "misses" unworthy of their titles to an Oriental mind. It sounded somewhat strange to hear that an American lady who was once married was introduced to me as "Miss Smith."

A "Miss" title in a genuine American sense is never restored to a Korean woman who was once married. She remains a widow or a divorcee all throughout her life unless she has an odd chance to marry again (This widow or divorcee is awkwardly called for convenience's sake "Miss" these days due to American influence if she works as an "office girl."). She is often referred to as "So-and-so's" mother, if she has any child. Even nowadays, Koreans address housewives mostly by using their child's name or by their husband's occupation title with or without his last name. But it is also notable that among peers they address each other by their first name, even after marriage.

The traditional Korean home is not that which is created upon marriage and disappears upon the death of a spouse, but that which has been inherited from remote ancestors and should be passed down to posterity in an uninterrupted line of succession. For this ultimate purpose a woman leaves her home to be a member of her husband's family. To marry is to leave her own home permanently. Once a daughter leaves her parents to go to her husband's home, she is not supposed to cross her father's door-step again. When the first marital quarrel takes place, the American concept of "running home to mother" is alien to traditionally minded Koreans. Modern young Korean wives, however, are beginning to learn to "run home to mother."

The tendency for Korean wives to assume self-independent identity has become more visible and vibrant, as they became more financially independent bread winners in the closing years of 1980s. It is reported that some 20 percentage of Korean wives hold a well paying job at private and public sectors, and, moreover, it is expected that more Korean women will want to work full-time for the betterment of their family life. If this tendency continues, so it may seem, the status of Korean women will be considerably improved, especially when the women's rights movement paves the way for their emancipation from the male-dominated society.

Traditionally, freedom is never given to young people in the process of mate selection. Marriage is arranged by the parents of each family, and its significance, unlike in the United States, lies not in bringing happiness to individuals based on affection and equality between husband and wife. Social life is not on the couple basis in the traditional Korean scheme of things. Korean society is centered around the father-son relationship, whereas American society is centered around the husband-wife relationship. In the father-son centered-society human relationship is carried on on a superordination-subordination basis. In the husband-wife centered-society, however, every human relationship is carried on on an equality basis.

In the traditional Korean system the continuity of the family through patrilineal succession from father to son was of the uppermost importance. The husband-wife relationship was of secondary importance. The wife was regarded as an outsider by her husband's relatives. The Korean wife was not and still is not given the surname of her husband upon marriage. She is the only one in the family who does not carry the surname of the family. This custom can be explained as evidence of the emphasis on the purity of the patrilineal blood line. The surname one takes from one's father stands for patrilineal origin. Prof. Choi (1975: 5) says that changing the surname breaks off one's relation with the patrilineal blood line.

A Korean wife was looked upon as a mere instrument giving birth to many sons for her husband's family in order to perpetuate their blood line. The status of women within the family was subordinate to men (The period when the predominance of man over woman was most pronounced was the Yi dynasty.). Women had no formal names other than the maiden name used informally at home only. In the Yi dynasty women were not entitled to social activity or legal action in their own right.

Regarding male superiority and female subordination, Lee O-Young (1967: 135) recalls a humorous story:

Once an American visited Korea before the Korean War and saw a scene on a mountain path in which a man was riding a donkey and his wife followed behind, panting. The American was startled and asked, "Hey, don't you know the proper way of treating women? Ladies first! Don't treat women so badly." Expressionless the Korean gentleman answered, "This is our custom."

However, when the American again visited Korea just after the Korean War, he saw quite an opposite picture. This time, on the same mountain path, the woman was riding a donkey in front and the man carefully followed far behind. The American thought this curious. He said "Hey, your customs have changed from before, haven't they?" But the gentleman replied without batting an eye, "I'm sorry. Since the war my wife goes in front because there are land mines buried all around here."

Prof. Ha comments that husband-wife ties during the Yi dynasty were characterized by a superordination-subordination relationship. Under the three basic principles of Confucian ethics, husband-wife relations were treated in parallel with the relations between king and subjects, or between father and son. The dominance of husband over wife was so strictly carried out that women were never self-assertive in domestic affairs. There is an old saying that when a hen crows, the house is doomed. Under these circumstances, the wife had to be blindly submissive to her husband in the belief that all a wife had to do was to follow her husband.

Traditionally, Korean women had been virtual slaves. Three kinds of obedience were demanded from a wife. That is, a woman had three masters during her lifetime—her parents when she was young, her husband when she married, and her son when she was old. Chastity was also strictly required. Women were not given freedom to go out of doors, and thus confined within the house. In the husband's case, however, he was rather free, and concubinage and polygamy were culturally approved. A Korean man, like a Japanese or a Chinese, could divorce his wife for any one of seven reasons (cf. Hatsumi 1965: 123) — if she did not obey his parents, if she did not bear children, if she committed adultery, if she was jealous, if she had an incurable disease, if she talked too much, and if she stole. On the other hand, women were not permitted to divorce their husband, nor was remarriage allowed. When the husband died, his wife was required to observe three years of mourning just as a son does upon the death of his father. The husband, however, wore a mourning dress for only one year when his wife died (It was equivalent to the mourning period parents observe for their children.).

Since the end of 19th century, the status and role of woman has changed a great deal in the home, in society and in the sphere of employment. According to Prof. Choi (1975: 10) the major factors affecting the changes in the status and role of women are: first, the equal opportunity for education since the end of 19th century; second, employment outside of the family circle and the conjugal family pattern (the nuclear family type) due to urban industrialization; and third, as an effect of family planning, Korean urban women on the average marry at an older age and have fewer children (Yoon 1971: 57) (The size of the family in the post-war years has been getting smaller, exemplified by the general desire for fewer children: today, parents want two boys and one girl.). Most modern Korean women complete their task of bearing and rearing children before they become 35, and when their last child goes to school, their golden period of leisure starts.

A modern Korean woman has still a lot of social disadvantages and discrimination compared with an American woman. There is an increasing desire among women to get jobs for their own self-development, but most Korean employers prefer men. It is almost impossible for women to preserve their jobs after marriage. The notion that a woman's role is to take care of domestic affairs at home is still strong. Male-centered social institutions strengthened by the Yi Dynasty still persist. The dominance of man over woman derived from Confucian authoritarianism is still deep-rooted.

Many people say that Korea is still a paradise for men. The most common complaint among housewives is that their husbands stay out very late every evening. After work Korean men, instead of going directly to their homes, often drop into their favorite hangout and drink with friends till the late hours. You would be more than a bit stunned by the scene downtown as men, linked arm in arm, stagger through the streets and everyone scrambles to catch the last bus or subway around 12 :00 P.M. Most of the time, Korean housewives must be patient and understanding.

During my short stay in America, I discovered that the domestic virtue of American men is the principal source of all their other good qualities. It functions not only as a promotor of industry, but also as the most powerful restrainer of public vice. This virtue reduces American life to its simplest elements, and renders happiness less dependent on precarious circumstances. I read somewhere that this domestic virtue of American men insures the proper education of children, and acts, by the force of example, on the morals of the rising generation; in short it does more for the preservation of peace and good order than all the laws made for that purpose; and is a better guarantee for the permanency of the American government than any written instrument, the constitution itself not excepted.

But the force of American domestic virtues is inseparable from the relatively powerful status of a wife in the structure of the American family. By considering their wife not only as an equal, but also as a superior in dealing with daily matters at home, American husbands make their family structure the living example of a democratic organization, for democracy is not just an equality, but an even distribution of relative merits and superiorities. Korean husbands, on the other hand, would never tolerate any challenge to their absolute authority and superiority from their wives.

2.4. SOCIAL-EMOTIONAL INTERACTIONS

As the family unit shifts from a large size to an atomized husband-wife core, and as women gradually come to claim status and rights equal to men in the political, economic, social and cultural fields, marriage places increasingly more emphasis on bringing happiness to individuals based on affection and equality between husband and wife. In the process of mate selection and marriage, much more freedom is now given to young people. In their social emotional interactions, however, Korean men and women are much more reserved than Americans.

Many times I was startled and embarrassed when I saw before my eyes young American men and women expressing their love openly in the streets or under the shade of trees or even behind mail boxes. It seems to me that American people from their early stage of life are so admirably and naturally well accustomed to and trained in expressing their emotions and passions that they take them for granted. It often stuns me into admiration to see how expressive Americans are of what they feel in their social-emotional interactions. When I visited an American campus for the first time, I can hardly remember now how many times my steps were arrested by the sight of American students' public display of affection. The expression of passions is not so free, love is not so warm and sweet in Korea as in the United States. The public holding of hands and dating is still foreign to many Koreans, and public display of affection is considered ridiculous and sometimes becomes a target of public scorn. When a Korean is overjoyed with something or when he faces sad things, it is a virtue to conceal his own feelings. A Korean wife never rushes to embrace or kiss her husband at a railway station or airport in public even when they meet after many years' absence. They love inwardly, suppressing passionate expressions. American couples' passionate kissing not only in public but also in presence of their own children would be shocking to Koreans. Expressions of love and hate are silently squashed instead of being stated. Once the love is bonded between a Korean husband and wife, it tends to remain being sticky amidst frequent family conflicts which often threaten its integrity and healthiness. Many Koreans seem to believe that the love between a husband and wife can be strengthened when they have a chance to overcome difficulties undermining it. A Korean couple prefer to sacrifice themselves to save the marriage when it is in danger rather than to solve it by leaving each other. Because of their belief in the marriage bond which was deeply rooted in Confusianism, Koreans are boastful of recording one of the lowest divorce rates among industrialized countries. In contrast, the love between an American couple is less enduring and relatively short tempered, just like a pad of steel which gets quickly heated, and yet gets cool over a short period of time. Although the intensity of their love is ultimately deeper than Koreans', as long as it gets the energy to be heated with, it wobbles in the nick of the time when the heat of love is somehow lost. For this reason, most American couples (as long as they stay married) look like they still have a crush on each other and thus give the impression of being very happy. In fact, they express their such amorous feeling in an overt way even in public. However, when the intensity of their love which bonds the couple together is lost for one reason or another, their marriage is apt to be abortive, and no one can save this troubled marriage. Moreover, it does not seem to be easy in every respect for American couples to maintain the same level of the intensity of love in the modern society as they did some decades ago, primarily because of distracting factors that are accumulating. As a consequence, the 20th century has witnessed an American ridden with the highest divorce rate in recent years.

In Korea, one does not usually praise another's kindness, generosity and hospitality. It is interesting to note that the Korean language does not have such expressions as "It is very kind of you"; "How generous of you", etc. Koreans deem this sort of expressions as flattering ones which one has to avoid using. The area of these language expressions calls for a special attention, because foreigners, who are not well adjusted to Korean culture and the use of the Korean language, may slip into carrying over English expressions into their use of Korean equivalents. But, all this does not mean that Koreans are different from other human beings. They certainly feel the same emotions and passions, the same jealousy, envy, joy, and happiness as Americans — only their external reaction to them is different.

This can be traced back to the traditional teachings of Confucianism that the expression of affectionate behaviors or gestures should not be permitted in the presence of others. Laughter should be abandoned before one's elders. Even a young mother was not free to express spontaneous love for her baby in front of her parents or elders. A husband should not praise his wife or son to others. A Korean common adage goes, "One who boasts of his son is half a fool and one who boasts of his wife is a complete idiot" (Kim 1975: 10). Those old teachings will run deep in the minds of Korean people, although Western influence and recent trends of residential separation between parents and young couples are slowly changing such traditional patterns.

Although modern younger couples are often seen walking side by side in the street or appearing at a social gathering or party, it is still considered silly and awkward for a husband to be accompanied by his wife. Traditionally, it is regarded as taboo for men and women to walk side by side in public. A woman's place is always a few paces behind her husband. When I first came to America I thought that there must be something wrong with the American idea of "ladies first." American men help their wives with the cooking, dish washing, laundry, etc. Such a thing would be absolutely unthinkable in Korea. It is taboo for men to do washing or cooking in the kitchen. American men also open car doors for women; they take their wives' coats to hang; they escort them when they go out. To Koreans American men appear "hen-pecked" husbands, whereas to Americans the Korean notion of male superiority would be utterly absurd.

Korea has also some peculiar sexual ethics. Sexual congress or marriage between relatives, close or distant, is a deep-rooted taboo. Marriage between relatives belonging either to the father's side or to the mother's side (except for those who stand beyond the mother's first cousins) is forbidden by law. The mere thought of marriage between relatives is repulsive and disgusting to Korean people. Marriage between relatives, however, happens not infrequently in Japan or in the United States. Marriage between cousins is not a rare event in Japan. In the case of one's brother's death, it has been also possible in Japan for one to marry his brother's wife in order to insure the succession of the family line. It is also possible in the United States for one to marry his second cousin. Such things would be absolutely unthinkable in a Korean situation. Crane (1967: 185-6) writes that the traditional strict sexual morality for women and the methods of protecting young girls from an over-emphasis on sex during their school years contrast with the tremendous sexual competition among young Western girls, the growing moral laxity, and the high percentage of divorces seen in Western countries. He stresses that this puritanical approach to sex in Korea has preserved the home and family system for thousands of years.

Korea today shows many faces. In cities and even rural areas, many social changes are happening in all levels of society. Young people now pattern their clothes, their hair styles, and their make-up after the latest fads seen in Western countries. The traditional strict sexual morality is giving way to modifications stimulated by increasing contacts with foreign cultures. The old traditions are being strongly influenced or challenged by those who have received advanced education in Western countries and by those Koreans who tread every corner of the earth to promote an export business. The increasing number of Koreans who have received higher education abroad have changed substantially in their basic ways of thinking and acting. The old ways of thinking, however, remain strong in the minds of most people, regardless of their education and foreign influence. It is not because of the overlay of Western dress and manners, as Crane remarks, that the inner man has changed. A mere superficial overlay of Western thought patterns has changed the outward appearance of many. In the thought patterns and attitudes of Korean Christians, they are in reality more Confucian and Buddhistic than Christian.

2.5. MANNERS AND GESTURES

Koreans burst into laughter or giggle where Americans would put on dead serious look in a corresponding situation. The Koreans' inscrutable smile might be misunderstood when trying to conceal anguish or enmity. Americans' shrugging of their shoulders to indicate a variety of responses is a puzzle to Koreans. When a Korean guest shows his appreciation of the fare by lustily slurping his soup or smacking his lips, an American host would clearly be scandalized.

Certain bodily gestures and manners that are typical of Koreans, such as belching, hawing, coughing, or hiccoughing appear outlandish or eccentric to Americans. But they are permissable, with the exception of blowing one's nose at the Korean dinner table. Belching after enjoying a meal indicates the gustatory satisfaction of a Korean guest. Hawing after having something to drink has roughly the same effect. In either case the host is assured that his guest is thoroughly enjoying the food or drink served. But quite the opposite is true in the United States. Americans have to excuse themselves each time they belch, cough or hiccough. Blowing one's nose, however, is permissible. I recollect one incident where I was bewildered when I witnessed an American blow his nose in public within a couple of months of my arrival in the USA. This incident occurred during the orientation led by the dean of the college for new foreign students for the fall semester. The room where the orientation was held was full of a group of staffs and a large number of foreign graduate students who came to solicit information about the regulations which the university set. Because it was a deadly cold winter, it was not unusual to hear many people coughing and sneezing due to colds. When the meeting was put into session, the dean, a tall and thin man, stood up in front of the whole class. Before he delivered his first word, he pulled an already dirty looking hangkerchief out of his pocket and heavily blew his nose a few times. By the time I thought that was over, he went on to fold it in half, blew his nose once again, folded that in its half, and finally slid it back into his pocket. As if it were a knee-jerk response, that scene turned my stomach into sour twist. I was not the only one who felt disgusted with witnessing this scene. I still vividly remember having seen grimaces creeping on the faces of many foreign students and their making growling noises as a sign of absorbing the apparent cultural shock.

Picking one's teeth after a meal is a well-known rule in Korea, whereas in America it is impolite and should be avoided until one is alone.

At a Korean dinner table, a young person waits until elders sit down and start eating. It is impolite to pick up his spoon before his father or grandfather begins to eat. In the presence of an elder, he does not smoke or drink. If he happens to be caught smoking, or an older person comes into his presence, he discreetly hides the cigarette behind his back. When drinking with an elder, a young man is discreet enough to hide his glass away, turning his body to drink. Even wearing glasses in the presence of an elder is sometimes con-

sidered impolite, especially in the rural areas. I remember very vividly that I was scolded very hard by my uncle for wearing glasses in
the presence of my father's friends who came to present their condo-
lences on the death of my father.

Korean people do not talk much, while eating. Good conversations
and the singing of songs, usually come after eating is done. An exception is when eating is combined with drinking, since in this case the
primary emphasis falls on socializing rather than eating itself. In
comparison, the scene of Americans eating is too noisy and self-
indulgent, and it is impossible to distinguish whether they are eating
or rehearsing a speech, or whether they are laughing or babbling, as
Lee O-Young puts it. In fact, one has to learn to distinguish chewing
or drinking from talking, so that one does not have to answer to
questions with a mouth full of food. For this reason, Americans tend
to take a relatively small amount of food at the dinner table. But in
Korea this would be a clear blunder: one has to show one's appreciation of the dinner by gorging oneself on it. It is not improper to make
noises while chewing or drinking soup at a Korean dinner table.
Koreans chew and drink audibly. In America, however, it is considered
improper to make noises while eating or drinking, although it is quite
natural to talk. On the other hand, many Koreans tend to think that
Americans licking their fingers, while eating hot dogs on the board
walk, is filthy and unsanitary. Foreigners can avoid a social gaffe by
taking time to master the proper Korean eating manner, including the
use of chopsticks .

To Koreans it is indelicate to use the hands to pick up food when
eating. They use spoons, forks or chopsticks. They even use a tooth-
pick to pick up strawberries or a piece of fruit. When I was faced in
an American home with a plate of crackers, I was at a loss what to do
with them.

My wife and I were once invited by my Arab friend to his home.
Having left his wife and his children behind in his country, he prepared all the food himself. He made several kinds of food out of cab-
bage, meat and rice. When we sat together at the table, my wife and I

were greatly surprised when my Arab friend began to take his food, using only his fingers to pick up food. He was exceptionally good at handling hot food using only hands instead of using chopsticks or spoons. At the sight of his greasy hands, I suddenly felt like stopping eating.

A gap between cultures is often too great. Americans take it for granted to eat beef but they are easily shocked at Koreans who enjoy eating dog-meat. In 1988 when Korea hosted the 24th Olympiad in Seoul, eating dog-meat by Koreans stirred up an international debate as to its cultural soundness. Since the culture of eating dog-meat is commonly practiced by other East Asian countries, I would like to introduce some interesting stories behind it.

Some hundred years ago, a French missionary couple were traveling with their pet dog, named "Kelly", through the northern part of China. After a long and dreary trip, they wanted to drop by a nearby restaurant for a meal, but it was not easy for them to find one where they were able to communicate with people in the restaurant either in French or in English. As luck would have it, after a couple of hours of search, they at last found one nice looking restaurant at a cozy town. When they stepped into the restaurant, the handsome waiter greeted them with beaming smiles, although his almost unintelligibly accented English made them wonder what he was trying to say. To their dismay, however, the waiter told them that they should not accompany the dog at the dining table, because Chinese culture predilects animals be separated from human beings, not to mention eating with humans at the table. Pretending to be courteous enough to abide by the culture of the country they are foreign to, they let the waiter take the dog Kelly away from them. When they settled themselves at the table, feeling much hungry, they ordered a couple of Chinese dishes, and also asked him to bring some kind of meat to the hungry dog. But this waiter who was very deficient in the command of English repeated with some inkling of doubt, "dog meat, dog meat, right?" Being a bit impatient and hasty, the French couple responded, "Right, dog meat, bring meat to the dog." About an hour later, the waiter placed on the table the ordered Chinese dishes and a lump of meat which they had neither seen nor eaten. When they discovered that it was Kelly they had cooked up, both almost fainted out of the chair. The husband fumed and burst into yelling, "Where is my Kelly?" In short, this story accentuates the importance of communication among people of different languages and cultures.

For another account, when Korean sponsored the 24th Olympiad in Seoul in 1988, several news media in the USA aired various special programs to highlight the cultural aspects of Korea—a country known as "the land of morning calm." The dog-meat culture of Korea, as the media reported it throughout the world network with live pictures of slaughtered dogs at the market, was one of the most controversial programs which provoked the Association for the Protection of Animals. The New York Times published a series of articles which severely criticized the dog-meat Korean culture as being barbarous. To some extent, the Korean news media launched as a repercussion the defense of eating dog-meat as a means for promoting national health. Although a debate of this nature lies beyond the present scope of this section, it suffices to mention that cultural identities are uniquely molded over a long period of time by the nation, which may defy any subjective judgment.

Beefeaters are considered barbarians or even cannibals by those who, like Hindus, never use beef as food. While Americans enjoy bacon and ham, Muslims regard pork as taboo food. Nowhere is the cultural difference more keenly expressed, than in the dietary norms set by different societies. Conversely, there is no better way to understand another culture than to learn to enjoy its delicacies.

Too often gestures cause misunderstanding and embarrassment, and a gap between cultures often shocks us. Ignorance of social usage can result in many blunders. In America shrugging one's shoulders with a slight movement of the hands upward means "I don't know", whereas a Korean way of "I don't know" is indicated by shaking one's head horizontally. By shaking their head, some people (living at the base of the Himalayas) react in the affirmative rather than in the negative.

I read with deep interest in the short essay contributed to the Korea Times by Prof. Kim Jai-Hiun that in the United States a Korean student was once brought to trial before a court on the charge of "shameless, demoralizing conduct directed toward innocent, preschool children", because he asked a small preschool boy to show his "pepper" (the reproductive organ). In Korean culture it is quite permissible to ask a boy to show his pepper to demonstrate that he is a boy, not a girl. Every Korean boy feels proud to show his pepper to grownups. This idea originated from Confucianism in which the domination of male over female had been well established. Not long ago, a similar incident was reported by the New York Times, which put into national disgrace many Koreans living in New York City. According to this newspaper, one day a Korean green grocer asked his customer's little boy to show him his little pepper, intending to indirectly show his friendliness to the long time customer by petting his child. This white customer, being ignorant of Korean culture, got into a fury and sued him for child sexual abuse for punishment in court. Representatives from the New York Korean community chan- neled their efforts to convince the jury that Korean culture was the major culprit. Luckily, he was acquitted of the sexual abuse case and was set free. But this incident brought home to the New Yorkers the importance of cultural understanding whose ignorance often traps them into such a predicament.

Just before my departure for the mainland after my stay at the University of Hawaii, my academic advisor came to the Honolulu Airport. She waved her hand vertically, palm outward. She meant by this "goodbye". But I took it as a signal "to come here", and so I hurried over to her to her embarrassment. Marking a circle with your thumb and your second finger indicates "money" in Korea, whereas this means a strong expression of "OK" in America. "Thumbing up" sig- nifies consent or "Okay" and "thumbing down" signifies "no" or disagreement, while in Korea "thumbing up" means "number one", or "boss" or "the best".

The use of the thumbs up or thumbs down gesture in the Western World to indicate something that is good or bad seems to have originated in the 19th century novels of ancient Rome. At least according to Bulwer-Lytton the thumbs up and thumbs down gestures were used during the gladiatorial games of ancient Rome. These gestures were used to indicate whether or not the life of the fallen gladiator should be spared. If the spectators gave a thumbs up the gladiator's life was spared, if the gesture was thumbs down the fallen opponent was slain. In a somewhat different tradition, American movie critics at times use "two thumbs up" in categorizing released movies into different ratings. In this case, the phrase means that movies receiving the "two thumbs up rating" are the best ones among the ones reviewed which they recommend people to watch.

Gestures are really embarrassing. At another time an American friend beckoned to me to come using the typical American gesture in which, with the hand in a palm upward position the index finger is repeatedly and rapidly pointed at the individual called and then flexed toward the caller. When this occurred, I became somewhat angry because I felt I was insulted. Such a gesture in Korea would only be used to threaten someone to come up or to call some inferior person or a child. In Korea the gesture to call someone consists of waving the hand with the palm down toward the person called. Often this gesture is confused by Westerners who think it means "good bye". This gesture is also used in Western culture to call a dog or a cat.

In one situation in a western novel (perhaps written by Emile Zola) when a suitor was questioned by the girl's father about his financial situation and his ability to support a wife, the young man replied by raising his hands above his shoulders and flexing his arms and saying, "I don't have much but I have these strong arms to protect and work for your daughter." Such a gesture would be unlikely to occur in Korea since raising one's hands in such a manner would be construed to be threatening to the older person. In Korea the young man would be more apt to point to himself and say, "I have these two strong testicles and I will work hard."

Another embarrassing "gesture" of sorts occurred in a college classroom during a Peace Corps volunteer's first semester of teaching. Too much noise in the back of the room prompted him to react as an American teacher might. He raised one finger to his mouth and hissed "shhhhhhhhh. . . His class litearlly broke up in laughter. It did not take him long to discover that such a sound is used in Korea to persuade a child to perform before the toilet.

The way Koreans and Americans use their hands and fingers to show sexual connotations is quite different. Pointing with one's middle finger is taboo in America whereas in Korea inserting a thumb between the second and middle fingers of the same hand or brushing the half-folded palm of one hand over the fist of the other hand implies sexual relations.

In another situation a young Korean high school student newly emmigrated to the United States was struck by one of his classmates when he was found rubbing his desk with his extended middle finger, unaware of the implied symbolism in American society. Since such a gesture has no meaning in Korea, he was at a loss to understand why he was struck. It wasn't until later that the meaning of the extended middle finger was explained to him by another Korean student. In America the use of this gesture is considered crude and extremely degrading to the individual since it implies that the individual can only have sexual intercourse with himself (or herself).

There is a custom, in America, of teasing a child by pretending to "steal" his nose. The "teaser" gently grasps the child's nose between index and middle finger and with a slight tug, pulls it away inserting the thumb between these two fingers exclaiming, "I got your nose." The thumb is displayed as being the nose of the child, and the desired reaction is one of at least pretended alarm on the part of the youngster. The first, and only time a Peace Corps volunteer did this in Korea it produced such a violent reaction on the part of the Koreans he was with that he was forced to learn what such a gesture means in a Korean cultural frame. The reaction is quite different from the one

Americans would have in an American cultural setting.

Misunderstanding of nonverbal communication of an unconscious kind is one of the most vexing, and unnecessary, sources of international friction. Consider, for example, the hands over-the-head self handshake of Khrushchev which he made in response to Americans' receiving him warmly when he came to America in 1959. Americans interpreted it as an arrogant gesture of triumph, as that of a victorious prize fighter, whereas Khrushchev seems to have intended it as a friendly gesture of international brotherhood. Would Pearl Harbor have occurred if Americans had been able to read the "Japanese smile" of the diplomats as they left their last fateful meeting with Secretary of the State Cordell Hull? (LaBarre 1976 : 227).

2.6. PRIVACY

I have heard Americans living in Seoul complaining that they are too often asked by Koreans about their personal matters such as "Are you married?" or "Are you a Christian?" or "How old are you?" Koreans' inquisitiveness about other people's private lives is usually motivated by their desire to seek a more intimate personal relationship or closer friendship. One may here note that section 1.5. alluded to the similar point that Koreans adopt an overly inquisitive manner to break through the barriers of privacy. Your age gives a Korean friend a cue as to "how to behave toward you." These questions, however, are a taboo in America, especially toward ladies.

An exchange Fulbright woman professor (who had just come to teach English literature at our university) was interviewed in my room by a student reporter of a school newspaper. One of the question was, "How old are you?". Although she was unhappy about the question, she gave the answer, "I'm thirty eight years old." This embarrassing question was followed immediately by some other stupid questions, "Are you married?" and "Why didn't you get married?" Then she blurted out somewhat angrily, "I have as much a right to remain single as to marry." To be exact, there is no concept of privacy in Korea. In Korean culture, an individual is not an isolated entity but a member of a group, within which he is exposed to constant concern or interference. Privacy is often ignored because Koreans tend to be too kind to others. How American privacy and Korean kindness interact in a personal relationship can be well demonstrated in a following example from a Peace Corps Volunteer's experience:

> After a long day at school, Sally often enjoyed sitting alone in her room reading, listening to music, or writing letters. Unfortunately, her Korean "sister" would always come in to talk with her, saying that it was too bad that Sally was so bored she had nothing to do but sit in her room by herself. Sally kept trying to explain that she was perfectly happy and she really wasn't bored, but her "sister" didn't seem to believe her. She continued to come to Sally's room whenever Sally was alone without asking her permission.

I was somewhat annoyed in an American home when a host or hostess talked too much while eating. Talking persistently to somebody at a dinner table distracts from the pleasure of eating. Americans never seem to understand that by indulging in excessive talk, they are really intruding on the private and personal pleasure of another's enjoying food.

An American friend once complained to me that he was often placed in an awkward predicament while doing business in a Korean public bathroom because its locking device was out of order. He said that he had to hold the door with one hand and a parcel of books with the other hand all the way while doing business. He was very much afraid of someone opening the bathroom door without knocking. I said to him that he should not have worried about that. Every discreet

Korean would "cough" before entering a bathroom or a private room. By clearing his throat, he calls attention to his presence. Coughing is a very gentle way of announcing oneself.

Koreans cough and Americans knock. Both coughing and knocking are used to respect the privacy of individual life. Because of the Western influence, city people in Korea have been using "knocking" as a method to announce themselves, but still it does not seem to have been completely absorbed in the Korean blood. My relatives from the country often stay at my home and "cough" instead of knocking when entering a bathroom. Sometimes their coughing is not audible enough to the person behind a bathroom door and they meet with disgrace.

The Korean way of announcing oneself seems to be more polite and gentle than the American style of knocking. I often find myself in an American office where somebody knocks loudly at the door and the person inside shouts "Come in." Knocking too often makes a man disturbed and annoyed, and the loud voice, "Come in" is very frightening as well. Loud knocking itself intrudes on one's privacy instead of respecting it. The act of knocking itself is already a loss of etiquette.

A Korean visitor does not knock; he coughs to announce his arrival. A discreet cough is enough to inform the person in his private room that an interruption is impending. The man inside slowly rises and puts on his clothes (a Korean often stays almost "undressed" at home), adjusting himself. Then they see each other and exchange greetings.

I still recall that my father would "cough" (or "ahem") as he passed in front of the door of the room where my elder brother and his new bride stayed. This coughing was intended as a way to signal his presence so that he might not embarrass his newly married daughter-in-law. My three year-old baby prefers to stay with my mother, and every morning my mother coughs clearly several times before entering the room with the baby, where my wife and I stay.

There is no difference between coughing and knocking in that both caution others to be careful that someone is approaching. But coughing seems to be a more quiet and subtle expression of warning than knocking. It is a rather indirect, warm suggestion. Knocking is so direct and overt an expression of caution that it often startles someone. Without speaking to each other, as Lee O-Young (1967: 52) puts it, Koreans employ a subtle gesture and a suggestion from heart to heart which avoids directness. It is a subtle form of communication which indicates the Korean mind. Coughing is like scorched rice tea (숭늉) (a typical Korean drink made from the scorched rice lying on the bottom of the pot in which rice was boiled. It is mixed with hot water and drunk following each meal), while knocking is really like bitter and tangy Coca Cola.

2.7. PREFERENCE FOR SONS

One day a friend of mine who had come to the University of Hawaii with me in the same year received a letter from his Korean family. His wife had been pregnant when he left. The moment he heard the news from his mother, "You have got a son," he was so overjoyed that he bounced up and down on the bed and uttered a wild cry several times. His American roommate was looking in surprise at the strange scene, wondering whether his Korean roommate had lost his mind. At this moment I entered their room and saw what had made my friend so crazy. I congratulated him and explained to his roommate what had happened to his Korean friend. He seemed not to fully understand the special significance "having got a son" has in Korean culture. I realized it was somewhat difficult to carry over the Korean cultural significance to a person whose culture places no more significance on "having got a son" than it does on "having got a daughter." That night my friend invited some of his

Korean friends and his roommate to a beerhall downtown and held a drinking party in honor of his new baby son.

It might be a universal wish of human beings that their number of male and female children be well proportioned. Suppose you have two or three girls in succession, it is very nice, of course, to have another girl, but slightly disappointing. The same is true of the opposite case. I read somewhere that there was once a period in English history when male issue was the really important event. But the once desired preponderance of male over female is not felt so strong either in English culture or in American culture as in Korean culture.

In the traditional Korean family system the concept of the family's continuity through patrilineal succession from father to son led to the strong desire for sons. To have a son was regarded as an absolute necessity to succeed the family line. The first obligation for a woman was to give birth to a boy for her husband's family. The primary goals of the traditional family were ancestor worship, the bearing of sons, and patrilineal perpetuation of the family.

The preference for sons persisted all through the history of Korea (Ha 1975: 51), but it was most conspicuous during the Yi dynasty. The idea of patrilineal continuity had far-reaching influence upon Korean society. Married life was meaningless unless the wife had a boy. Many women were divorced because they failed to bear sons. Failure to bear a son was one of the seven conditions for expelling a wife which was generally accepted not only in Korea but also in China and Japan. The first condition to drive away a wife was disobedience to parents-in-law, and the second was barrenness. It was remarkable to note that failure to bear a male was regarded as a vice next only to disobedience to the husband's parents.

During the Yi dynasty many women who were unable to give birth to male children had to employ every means and device imaginable, including the offering of sacrifices to spirits. All the responsibilities for not bearing a boy went to women so that sonless mothers suffered all kinds of humiliation and discrimination. A sterile woman visited shrines hoping to have a son. Many a woman was forced to commit suicide. Much of the responsibility for Korean woman's low status and miserable fate can be ascribed to the preference for sons practiced so long in Korean society.

If one word expresses the essence of the Confucian moral and social order, it is filial piety (Lee 1976: 21-6). The father-son relationship and filial piety were of utmost importance in all family relations. Confucianism, with its emphasis on relationships, is one of the chief factors which have determined traditional Korean patterns of thought and action. Prof. Choi says that there are five cardinal articles of morality involving the relationship of father and son, master and subject, husband and wife, elder brother and younger brother, and friends (Choi 1975: 5). Filial piety meant that children had to be absolutely obedient to their parents and serve them and please them not only during their life time, but even after their death. It was a son's duty to provide old age security for his parents and then to look after them after death through the practice of the family memorial rites, "Chesa." The son's function of performing ancestor worship, continuing the family lineage and of achieving honor and wealth for the family as well as for oneself was the Confucian virtue of filial piety. Family ancestor worship, has been regarded as one of the most basic and important factors of the patrilineal Korean family. It is still observed extensively both in rural and urban areas.

During the Yi dynasty, men whose wives failed to give birth to a son were encouraged to keep concubines. Similar instances can be frequently seen around us recently. In the traditional Korean family, absence of male offspring meant not only an unpardonable act of impiety to one's forefathers but also a discontinuance of the family blood line which made the performance of ancestor worship impossible. Thus the custom of keeping concubines became widespread in parallel with the growth of boy preference. Not long ago some men were known to keep concuvines, in addition to their legal spouses, in their zeal to have a son. The custom of keeping concubines exerted a bad impact upon the Korean family. Polygamy itself reflects the dominance of men over women. Some men who could afford to keep concubiness, had little restraint in having them, even if their wives gave birth to many sons. They preferred living with young concubines rather than with their wives who had grown old by bearing many children. Living with the concubine gave rise to a lot of headache and trouble inside the family, as you can well imagine.

Even today in many Korean families, parents' attitude toward their sons is quite different from toward their daughters. There is a big difference in the recovery period when mothers give birth to daughters and when they give birth to sons. Clear distiction between sons and daughters can be felt in the depth of parental love, in clothing, bedding, and even toys. Different attitudes also exist when children make mistakes or quarrel with one another. Parental scolding usually goes toward daughters when sons are to be blamed.

As we have seen, Confucianism in Korea made a great contribution but it also produced some serious evils as well. Generation by generation and sex by sex, Koreans build many barriers in their minds because of which they cannot communicate their thoughts to others, whereas in America each individual personality is fully developed and recognized without strict age or sex classification. At any rate, Confucian authoritarianism still permeates every aspect of life in Korea despite Western influence. There is no Korean who is not concerned lest his lineage becomes extinct in his generation. Such an attitude consequently leads him to the idea of preferring sons for succession rather than daughters and observing "Chesa" which symbolizes the continuation of the lineage as unavoidable (Choi 1975:11).

2.8. DIFFERENT ATTITUDES TOWARD AGE

In my efforts to compare and contrast Korean and American life, I have found no differences that are greater than in the attitude towards age, which is distinct and admits of no intermediate positions. Strictly speaking, the differences in American and Korean attitudes toward drinking manners, toward hospitality, toward friendship, toward women and toward love are more or less all relative. The basic relationship between husband and wife is not different from that in America, nor even the relationship between parents and children. Not even the attitude toward sons and daughters in Korea is essentially so different from that in America. But in the matter of Korean and American attitudes toward age, the difference is greater than in anything else. Koreans and Americans take exactly opposite points of view. This is more or less true of China and Japan whose spiritual and cultural patterns of life and thought are largely based upon Confucianism.

When I studied at the University of Hawaii, my academic advisor was an old, retired English Professor, Dr. Elizabeth Carr. All of the participants were struck by her enthusiasm, deep devotion and her unfailing health. So at the end of the fall semester I said to her, "I would like to extend my sincere thanks to you for the enormous help and enlightening guidance you gave us in spite of your great age." Suddenly she put on a serious look, and I saw a portion of her mouth twisting. I had an inkling that she seemed unhappy about the way I expressed my thanks to her. Understandably enough, I was not a little embarrassed. A few hours later she told me that my remark "in spite of your great age" had reminded her suddenly that she was very old. I felt as if I had committed a big crime.

On my way to the University of Michigan (Ann Arbor), I stopped over in San Francisco for a few days. One day I went downtown shopping. Just before entering an elevator, I said to a respectful old man, "After you." He stood aside, saying to me with a smile, "After you," and so I blurted out "After age," forgetting that American people hate to be thought of as old. The old man entering the elevator, retorted half jokingly to me, "Do you think you are younger than me?" Although he spoke jokingly to me, I felt ashamed.

With the full knowledge that American people do not like to be considered old, I restrained myself from commenting on age any more. But the Korean attitude toward age is quite different. To Korean people, growing old is in a way a sign of grace, respect and piety. Age is the first consideration when we communicate with one another. An individual in Korean society is designated a corresponding social status, among others, according to one's age. Age is the fundamental principle of social interactions in Korea.

Korean people are quick to respond to your age. Your age directs their behavior toward you. If you report a higher age than that of the inquirer, he immediately drops his voice in humility and respect. When you become acquainted with a Korean, he tends to become inquisitive about your age. He wants to know your age so that he may decide how to behave toward you. I have heard Americans living in Seoul complaining that they are too frequently annoyed by being asked their age.

Different attitudes and honorifics are employed according to whom you are speaking. There is little concept of equality among Koreans. A person whose age is greater than the speaker himself should be addressed in polite forms. It is almost impossible to carry on a conversation even for a few moments without taking age into consideration. Although one could use kinship terms such as "elder" or "younger" to indicate the order of seniority, the terms "brother" and "sister" in English do not themselves indicate age difference. But Koreans' counterparts signify the age difference in themselves such as "hyəŋ" (형 elder brother) or "Dongsɛŋ" (동생 younger brother). There is no term for just "brother" That is, a brother in Korea had to be either older or younger than oneself. "Even twins are not equal; the first one to show his face is senior and superior in position to the later one out" (Crane 1967: 13).

So, the latter has to address the former as "형 (older brother)," whereas the former has to address the latter as "동생 (younger brother)". Thus, the American way of addressing one's older brother by "Bob" or "Tom" never happens in a Korean situation "except when the addresser is still sufficiently young to be allowed to stray from the rule in terms of linguistic etiquette" (Park 1975: 4). The Korean older brother, therefore, is always addressed as "hyəŋ" or "hyəŋ-nim." The added particle "nim" turns "hyəŋ" into a more polite way of expression, which is used by grown-up brothers.

Koreans are so age conscious that the uses of kinship terms like "hyəŋ" or "hyəŋ-nim", "ənni" (언니, sister), "ajumoni" (아주머니, aunt) are usually extended beyond the family circle in Korea. In interpersonal communication, people of no actual blood relationship are frequently referred to through these kinship terms to show one's affection. For example, a close friend of one's brother, or one's senior in school days is addressed as "형" or "형님" with or without his first name preceding it. A close friend of one's sister is commonly called "언니." The father and mother of one's close friend are addressed as "apəji" (아버지 or 아버님, father) and "əməni" (어머니 or 어머님, mother) respectively. "Ajumoni" or "halmoni" (할머니 or 할머님, grandmother) depending on age, are used, in an ordinary conversation. In American culture, the words "uncle" and "aunt" are frequently used as well, but their use is generally restricted to intimate family circles, and when used, these words are always accompanied by personal names as in "Uncle Tom" or "Aunt Linda."

A teacher at a Korean grade school would always be considered as a person who should be respected not just because of his superior knowledge in his subject area, but even more so because of his older age. In contrast, even children in an American elementary school would address their teachers as a "Mr" or a "Miss," which can be quite shocking for a Korean teacher. As one goes up the American educational ladder, student-teacher relationships progressively become an equal-level interaction. For instance, you would find graduate students calling their professors "John" or "Bill" rather than "Professor." Although it could be safer to address a professor you do not know very well by using his last name with a title of doctor (e.g., Dr. Smith), professors and graduate students see each other as colleagues engaged in academic studies in which they have common interests. At Korean universities, even after a former student becomes a fellow faculty member of the department to which his former professor belongs, he would always have to pay full respect to his teacher. One's former teacher in a Korean school remains a teacher for one's life time.

I was unhappy to hear my first name mentioned frequently by an American roommate when a remarkable degree of intimacy had not yet been established. As months went by, I realized that American people often use first names in an informal situation to set others at their ease. For most Korean adults, however, calling someone by the first name, outside the circle of one's boyhood friends or classmates, never happens. To Koreans, a given name is something sacred and should be honored and respected, and should not be used casually. A

Korean treats his given name as if it were his own personal property. In most cases, the addressee's title is required. The facility with which most American adults go about first-naming their acquaintances, business colleagues, relatives and others, would be out of place in most of the corresponding Korean situations. Calling someone directly by his name is an affront to his person in most social circumstances. Not to use the personal names of elders or acquaintances is the rule in Korean culture.

The multistrata system of honorifics in a Korean context has no parallel in the English language, though the latter has its own way of indicating various social levels. Professor Song says that paraphrasing would solve some of the problems of sociolinguistic stratification. But the original flavor would be lost (Song 1969: 11). Korean people are so age conscious and the various social levels of speech employed by young persons in speaking to older persons are so complex that they cannot be rendered in corresponding English. Even the response to one's friend's question, viz. "Where are you going?" varies in Korean from age to age, i.e., in pre-adult level, the response might be "hakkyo-ey-ka-un-ta" ((나는) 학교에 간다), in adult level, "hakkyo-ey ka-a" ((나는) 학교에 가아), in mature level, "hakkyo-ey ka-ney" ((나는) 학교에 가네), and so forth.

Close friends use plain words with each other, whereas acquaintances tend to communicate in polite forms until they come into more intimate relationship. An adult speaks down to a child, whereas a child speaks up to an adult. C. Paul Dredge says that the first choice a Korean speaker must make is based on age and is almost invariably unconnected to any consideration of the power-authority dichotomy (Dredge 1976: 6). When a child grows to adulthood, his deference to those older than himself is still a continuing fact, regardless of the lack of influence an older person may actually have over him. Even an elderly beggar is addressed in very polite forms.

A Korean likes to use the expression, "I will be sixty the day after tomorrow," which literally does not mean that he will be actually sixty the day after tomorrow but figuratively means that he will be sixty in a couple of years. By saying this he demonstrates that he knows better about life than you do. The other connotative meaning is that "How fast time flies!" and I am now almost sixty, and I have a lot of things to do yet before reaching that age. This is based upon the oriental philosophy that a man is wiser as he grows older. An older man has crossed more bridges than a younger one. Thus, a Korean father lecturing his son must stop suddenly and change his demeanor the moment the grandfather opens his mouth.

No one doubts the wisdom of an old man. The traditional image of an old man to Korean people is that he enjoys the latter part of his life, surrounded by his sons and daughters and his grandchildren, which is the symbol of ultimate earthly happiness. He gently strokes the flowing white beard coming down to the breast and smiles in peace and contentment, "dignified because he is surrounded with respect, self-assured because no one ever questions his wisdom and is kind because he has seen so much of human sorrow" (Lin 1972: 66). This is why the people in Korea, as in other parts of Asia, take respect for older persons for granted, a notion which might seem unusual to American people.

The number of Korean old men with white beards is decreasing in number especially in urban areas. The wearing of a beard is indeed the special prerogative of those who have grown old with wisdom. A young man wearing a beard without the necessary qualifications is usually in danger of being sneered at behind his back.

Seniority really counts in every social activity in Korea. The wage scale in almost any institution or business organization directly reflects "hobong" (base salary) or the number of years one spent in the particular place where one worked. When a person is chosen as chairman or president at a social meeting, the first thing to be considered is his seniority rather than his personal ability. Even in a general election, when the result of the poll happens to be a draw, the final honor goes to the older person.

A Korean man in his middle age looks forward to his sixty-first birthday. He will be surrounded by his sons, daughters, and grandchildren, and his sixty-first birthday will be celebrated with great pomp and glory. In Korea, a man's sixty-first birthday (hwan kap) is celebrated as one of the most important festive occasions in his lifetime. The English word "sixty-first birthday" can hardly convey the emotion and sentiment the word "hwan kap" conjures up in a Korean mind.

After his sixty-first birthday a Korean old man does not have to work for a living. He has a good son taking his place and is honored to be fed by him. He has toiled for his children in his youth. He lost many a good night's sleep when they were ill, and spent almost his whole life bringing them up. Children's debts to their parents cannot be numbered. Korean parents, having taken good care of their children for a life-long time, are justly in turn taken care of by their children. Korean parents are now entering into a mellower season of life, and what they have lost in flowers they will more than gain in fruits. They will not only be loved and respected but also served with the best food and their favorite dishes. There is no shame attached to the circumstance of their being served by their children in the sunset of their life.

Koreans' respect for old age is also reflected in their attitude toward nature. Kim (1975: 9) beautifully describes the following:

> It is no coincidence that the majority of Koreans like autumn best while most Americans prefer spring. It would be interesting to know the reason for the difference in preference. Americans in general think of spring as a time of warmth and beauty and newness of life following the cold, dark, death-like winter. Philosophically speaking, spring is looked upon as the time of youth and autumn as the time of old age. Since Americans generally consider youth as the best time of life and accept old age with reluctance, perhaps this has something to do with their preference for spring. The innately emotional Koreans like autumn with its colored leaves falling in preparation for winter; similarly the older person preparing for death is revered.

Thus, the older you are, the more you are respected in Korea, and the golden period in your life lies not in youth, but lies ahead in old age. It is because of this premium generally placed upon old age in Korea that young men tend to report a higher age or try to pass themselves off as older than they are by imitating the pose and dignity and point of view of the older people. One often hears in Korea young men advising like old men others of the same age. But there is one exception to this rule. Understandably enough middle-aged single women never tell their true age. They are eagerly looking forward to the days when their Romeos come along and pick them up. But the years are slipping by mercilessly and they are seized with a gate-shutting panic, the fear of being left out in the dark when all the gates close at night. She remains twenty-nine for many years until she is happily matched to her man.

The whole Korean concept of life is based upon mutual help within the home. The little Korean baby on his mother's back is a good symbol of the whole cyclical Korean idea of family. The mother carries the baby on her back while he needs her in his infancy, and he, in turn, will carry her and his father on his back when they need him in their old age. This is a never-ending cycle of security and sacrifice, sacrifice and security. The duties of a son serving his parents are indeed rather severe as the words of the Buddha go: "It would be impossible for a son to repay his parents for their gracious kindness, even if he could carry his father on his right shoulder and his mother on his left for one hundred years."

Crane (1967: 188) comments on the strong family loyalties in Korea: The internal security in the family setup means that, with family backing, one can have a refuge from the storms of life. Among Korean children there are relatively few personality problems, as compared with the many problems of Western children who visit pediatric clinics. A child grows up riding on his mother's warm back, having food available at the nearest breast, and knowing that he will not be left alone in the darkness of a lonely room. He will sleep in security with his family. The family unit is more important than the individual. Decisions are made in favor of the family, rather than for the sole benefit of a single member. Family life in the West has much to learn from the Korean family pattern.

I still remember once reading Mrs. Linda Jo Banks' fine essay contributed to the Korea Times. She says that the prototype of the parent carrying the child and the son in turn carrying the parent, can be also seen in the West. There is a moving scene in the Aeneid, for example, where the Trojan Aeneas tells the story of the burning of Troy by the Greeks. The moment the flames break out, he rushes to the home of his aged father, Anchises, places the old man on his back, and tries to take out his wife and son at the same time through the hell-like burning city. Finally, he is able to save his father and his son, but his wife is forever lost to him. He later admits that he never once glanced back to see what was happening in the city, and though he grieves over the death of his wife, he never seems to feel guilt for what he had done. His first responsibility was always to his aged father and his son.

The concept of the personal obligation of children toward their parents, still so alive in Korea, seems to have become dull in modern, socialized American life. As the Korean family has been changing toward the pattern of the nuclear family system as an outcome of the urban industrialization process, the resulting situation frees the individual from the ties and burdens of the extended family. In regard to married children's attitude toward their parents in old age, however, nearly all replied in the recent urban family survey (1968) that taking care of aged parents should be the responsibility of the sons (cf. Korea Journal, Vol. 15 No. 11 November, 1975, p. 10).

The Korean pattern of family life would be intolerable to American people. In the blood of Americans, the insatiable desire of independence and freedom runs deep. American babies away from parents either play in a public nursery or amuse themselves happily on the floor instead of on their mothers' backs. Headstrong teenagers start dating at fourteen or fifteen and select their own mates while still young without taking into account their parents' wishes or judgment. As soon as they establish their own homes, they love their own privacy so much that they cannot tolerate the idea of living with their parents who have done so much for them. So too, old Americans generally prefer to live independently of their children and grandchildren, continuing their own lives, seeking their own interests and friendships among their own generation.

This American individualism makes the idea of growing old repulsive. They wish to leave the impression that they are still active and vigorous. I can now fully understand American men and women shrinking from telling their age because the whole pattern of American life places a premium upon youth. They insist on being busy and active until they are reduced to being taken care of by the government and society. America is a land for the young in every respect. Just think of the retired people painfully trying to look and stay young in Florida or Southern California. The old have to imitate the young in America, while the exact opposite seems to be true in Korea.

American culture has devised many elaborate systems to provide for those who are old, such as social security payments, medicare reimbursements, private retirement plans, retirement homes, transportation benefit and clubs. The American government and society take over the duty of the children. In short, the American government and society perform the same function for their senior citizens as Korean children do for their parents. But still there is something cold and unsettling to the soul in this American system when I see old people, away from their children, living a solitary life in retirement homes. How can the devoted personal service and respect and adoration of loving children ever be replaced by even the best housemaids or waiters or waitresses?

I have seen many older Americans effacing themselves and preferring to live alone in some retirement house or hotel with a restaurant on the ground floor, out of consideration for their children and an entirely unselfish desire not to interfere in their home life. They seem to love their independence so much that they count it their shame to be dependent upon their children. But among the many human rights man should keep as invaluable and sacred, the American people have pitifully forgotten about the right to be fed by their children in the sunset of their life.

It is not shocking at all to me when I recently read a piece of an article dealing with the newly emerging tendency that many old American parents want to live together with their offspring. According to the article, in the wake of a shrinking social benefit system at the turn of the 1990's, retired American people prefer to spend time helping their grown-up children, while they stay in their house. They think that exercising by doing things will enable them to stay healthy until their life expires. On the other hand, their children, in a sense, are in a position to welcome their old parents' assistance in baby sitting, taking care of nitty gritty chores, etc., primarily because more than 60 percentage of American middle class families have to work full-time in order to maintain the same standard of living as was made possible by a single income (usually a husband's income) 10 years ago.

2.9.   INTERPERSONAL INTERACTIONS

Korean life is controlled by two major contrasting forces: the Positive (陽) and the Negative (陰), Light and Dark, Good and Evil, the philosophy of which originated from Confucianism. According to the actual situation, this concept can be extended as male and female, king and ministers, father and son, husband and wife, older and younger, mother-in-law and daughter-in-law and so forth. These balancing opposites, if in proper relationship, fit together to form the perfect circle which means harmony or health, full maturity or round character. This idea of balancing opposites to form the perfect circle is well expressed in the Korean flag (태극기), the upper part of which is the fiery red male (陽), and the lower part of which is the soft blue female (陰).

The Positive (陽) is "aggressive, fiery, hot, dry, the south side of the mountain," whereas the Negative (陰) is receptive, regressive, quiet, soft, moist, swollen, the north side of the mountain. Any imbalance between these opposing forces surely causes disharmony. One of the basic differences between Eastern and Western cultures is that the Eastern is dominated by the concept of harmony

In the Positive and Negative oriented mentality, every human relationship is always centered around the thoughts of somebody else. One always feels the presence of another person. One cannot stand on one's own feet without thinking of the other. A man owes his success to his father or even his dead ancestors. He also ascribes his failure to something or someone else rather than to himself. He is linked from his father and dead ancestors down to his sons and those coming after them. Security in governmental positions or in business depends on having friends or fellow alumni holding higher and stronger positions.

An American would not tolerate the mere idea of counting on someone to do something for him. He rather prefers to do something in his own way without depending on others. While in America each person is respected as an individual, in Korea all human relations are deeply affected by the consideration of others. A Korean seems to be more concerned about how others regard him than how he regards himself. In this human relationship, there arises the so-called custom of "face" (체면) and "outside show" (겉치레). Because of the fear of the opinions of others, a Korean woman becomes a chaste widow or a dutiful wife. She is worried about what others think of her rather than what she thinks of herself. The prevailing Korean attitude about people is not usually individualistic or democratic; rather it tends to be paternalistic and feudalistic.

A Korean with a developed sense of "nunchi" (눈치) (Analysis of the attitudes and emotions of another person so that you may know how to respond) is always too sensitive to others. Different attitudes and honorifics are used according to whom he is speaking. He attaches such great importance to the feelings of others that he employs with subtlety different levels of deference according to whom he is speaking. By employing different levels of honorifics, the Korean language tells so clearly who the participants are in interpersonal communication that it often leaves out subject and object noun phrases without causing any ambiguity. Different speech levels realized in various verb endings reveal different participant relationships. Hwang Juck-ryoon (1975: 20) demonstrates a good example from a play in Korean:

(Participants: Mr. Song, a young man; Mr. Oh, Song′s friend; Miss Yu, Song′s girl friend)

Song: katani? chikum mya tsinte kantako kurana? (1)
(가다니? 지금 몇신데 간다고 그러나?)
going now what time go say ′What do you mean you want to go? You can′t say you are going when the night is still young.′

Yu: kurasil piryo ə pso-yo. Cheka kakets ə yo. (2)
(그러실 필요 없어요. 제가 가겠어요.)
do so need there is no I will go ′There is no need for that. I′ll go.′

Oh: o kuraesa ya twae-pnik-ka? (3)
(오 그래서야 됩니까?)
Oh, do do inappropriate ′Oh′ that′s not proper.′

Song: a waetul kuraeyo. kunyang ta tul iss-ə yo. (4)
(아 왜들 그래요. 그냥 다들 있어요.)
Ah, why do so as it is all stay ′What is all this about? Both of you just stay.′

Oh; kur ə chiman ir ə ke sessi pulpy nhachi an-a.　　(5)
(그렇지만 이렇게 셋이 불편하지 않아?)
but thus three or us uncomfortable ′but isn′t it uncomfortable for three of us to stay like this?′

Prof. Hwang goes on with a detailed explanation of the above utterance:

In (1) we can tell Song is addressing his male friend, because he is using the -**na** ending which is typically used between adult male friends. If he were addressing his girl friend, he would be using **kurae** or **kurae-yo** depending on the degree of intimacy and his personal style. The honorific infix "si" in kura-si-1, the yo′s in ə psoyo and kakess ə yo, and the humble form of the first person pronoun **che** shows that in (2) Miss Yu is addressing Mr. Oh rather than her boy friend. (In this case, however, the context is a surer clue because she might use the same deferential language to her boy friend depending on the degree of intimacy and her personal style.) The fact that Oh is using the formal and deferential −pnita ending in (3) shows that he is addressing Miss Yu, not his chum. Similar analyses would apply to (4) and (5).

Another good example of how the language reflects the stratification of interpersonal relations in Korean society is seen in the way a man refers to his wife. This is an example used by Paul S. Crane: The word "wife" which he uses will depend on his relative position to the one with whom he is speaking. For example, she is his "cho" (처) when speaking upward to a higher ranking person. To an equal, she is his "chip saram" (집사람) or his "an saram" (안사람), "house person" or "inside person." To an intimate friend, she may be his "anae" (아내). To a lower person, she is his "agi omoni" (아기 어머니), his "child's mother." Many Western men make the humorous mistake of giving honor and equal position to their wives in speaking Korean. Koreans feel that this is being presumptuous, is in poor taste, and at best a ridiculous mistake in the use of the language.

The speakers of English who believe in the innate equality of all men, interpreted the duality of the pronoun of address (thou/thee and ye or you) as a negation of that equality and with their democratic notions gave up the pronoun differentiation based upon social status. Personal pronouns in Western languages are universal indicators of human beings in the abstract sense, whereas in Korean they are particular markers of minute social differentiation between individuals.

Americans who have studied the Korean language to a certain extent and lived in Korea for an extended period of time may easily notice that the language is marked with sexism. For example, when the Korean instructor of the Korean program at American universities tries to explain various ways in which one can address one's own wife and other's, most American students burst into laughter, because to them all terms used for addressing the word "wife" sound downgraded, as if she is being looked down upon by the society as a whole. They think that the Korean language reflects a differential treatment for the words "husband" and "wife," which is sexually biased.

Among Positive and Negative philosophy oriented people, the first and foremost consideration tends to be something greater or larger than oneself. This is well reflected in the order in which Korean people put their family names first and then their given names last and write their mailing addresses, proceeding from a larger unit to a small unit, e.g. their country (or province), the name of the town, the local street name and number, and then their names last in order. Americans place their names or addresses completely the other way around.

The way Koreans and Americans write their names and addresses reflects some basic differences in their value and behavior judgments concerning themselves. Koreans tend to regard family or community or nation as the core center whereas Americans value themselves as the center. The way Americans attach priority to those things closest to themselves reflects how they value themselves relative to others. Americans tend to be self-assertive in doing everything. By placing their given names first they want to identify themselves as unique individuals on the earth different not only from other people but also from close relatives including immediate families. Interestingly enough, American first names are chosen from a relatively limited repertoire(e.g., John, Peter, Ann, Mary, etc.), whereas their family names no doubt reflect their immigrant ancestors' diverse cultural background and thus have virtually unlimited varieties. An average American is likely to run across many people who have the same given name as his or hers. In contrast, most Koreans, with widely used family names such as Kim, Lee, Park, Choi, Hwang, etc., may appear to a Westerner to be distant relatives and cousins.

A Korean often says "our wife" instead of "my wife." Foreigners will wonder, "With how many husbands is the wife living now?" He will continue to say "our house" instead of "my house," and "our country" instead of "my country." A Korean political leader will invariably declare with pride, "I am working hard for "our community" or "our country" or even our president." He will never say, "I am working for myself or my family." A Korean soldier will shout when asked for what he is having such a hard military drill or fighting, "I am fighting for 'our fatherland' or 'His Excellency." In a similar situation an American soldier will answer, "I am fighting for my home, or my dear love or my father and mother or my sister and brother or my dog and cat or my garden or my schools and churches which I attended." I guess American soldiers found it hard to discover the right answer as to what they were fighting for in the Vietnam war.

An American refers to himself in daily conversations as a proud "I" whereas a Korean either omits "I" in most cases or refers to himself as humble little being (제가 or 소인이) (manners in Korea are based on making oneself small and unobtrusive). On this Lee O-Young (1967:115) makes some comments: "Korean society is a totality in which 'I' is buried within 'We.' We have lived like a dog on a leash, pulled along by fate or our blood relatives or power. We have not discovered the actual sense of the "I" which determines our independently individual sense."

The basic concepts and codes of interpersonal relationships of Confucian ethics (e.g. ministers toward king, loyalty; son toward father, filial piety; wife toward husband, obedience) run deep in the blood of the Korean people. One is always more powerful than the other. One is always older than the other. One is always lower in rank than the other. Even among friends, some feel inferior to the others. All are in relatively higher or lower positions. One's respect and loyalty toward someone who is older and higher in rank is absolute. Anyone who breaks this rule is quite rude (상놈: "unperson"). President Park is often referred to as "His Excellency", whereas the American president is called "Clinton" or "Mr. Clinton." Human relationships are completely vertical in every walk of Korean life rather than horizontal. There is really little concept of equality in everyday interpersonal interaction.

Peaceful human relationships are well maintained among those belonging either to intimate groups or ingroups (e.g. relatives, friends, alumni, academic or religious groups) or to hierarchical groups (e.g. senior-junior, older-younger, higher-lower in positions). Koreans have been traditionally well trained under the teachings of Confucianism in how to get along well with each other in ingroups or hierarchical groups, but they have never been taught how to interact with those belonging to "outgroups." This is why Korean people are very strict in observing the rules of etiquette in personal relationships with those they consider as "familar." They are very much afraid to give the impression to their groups that they are rude or "brazen faced." Losing one's face is really fatal to smooth human-relationships. Koreans are so sensitive to relationships and politeness that they shy away from major conflicts with their ingroups. Every effort is made to remain within the framework of polite relationships.

Once polite relationships, however, are broken, Korean people start finding faults even with those belonging to their own groups, and tend to go wild and resort to violence. So long as you stay within "the ingroup of human relationship", you are secure and protected. It is very difficult for an outsider to penetrate the wall of the ingroup in Korean society. Korean people are rather exclusive to those they do not know well. It is much easier to approach an American than a Korean. But once you break down the wall of impenetrability, a Korean friend too easily gives his mind away.

To approach an American is one thing and to know him well is quite another. This kind of relationship is something like the structure of the Korean house and that of the American house. The Korean house with a strong wall and a huge gate is much more difficult to break into than a wallless American house. But once you succeed in entering into the house, you can more easily gain access to every room inside the Korean house than to the rooms of an American house, which are usually locked from the inside for privacy. It is perhaps for this reason that Americans need to talk to psychiatrists, with whom they feel safe to share their most private thoughts and feelings. A Korean, on the other hand, would call up his crony when he is troubled by personal anxiety. Thus, the cure would come from the shared talk and drink, the latter serving, as it were, as the prescribed medicine.

Koreans tend to be indifferent toward outgroups or strangers. When I came to an American campus for the first time, I was really impressed with the way American students greet each other with a smile, saying "Good morning", "Hi", "How are you?", etc., when passing by. I was really embarrassed when a beautiful girl said to me with a broad smile, "Good morning" when I was hurrying to my classroom. So I said to her, "I am afraid you mistake me for someone else."

The facial expressions of Korean people are usually fixed and rigid when they meet with persons they do not know, but they suddenly melt into soft, warm smiling expressions when they meet their intimate friends. Koreans are indeed affectionate and close to the persons they know well, but to the general public they are unexpectedly unfriendly and cold. This does not mean that they ignore or are hostile to people in outgroups. Some foreigners perceive the firm facial complexion of Koreans as people of an uncivilized and hostile personality. When they interact within ingroups, they are friendly and courteous, but you get a completely different impression of those you meet on the street. With regard to this matter, Lee O-Young (1967: 102) remarks:

> When we read Western novels, there are often scenes of strangers talking together of love; but in Korean novels there are almost none. The plots are between friends and the stories are about people who know each other quite well. As proof let's look at the comments of Clifton Fadiman on the novels of Dostoevski. The characters generally meet on the street. They drink a glass of liquor and like intimate friends they open up their inner thoughts and tell stories and confess everything about their lives.

The age-old cliche, "Koreans are the most courteous people in the

East" is rather rightly applied only to inter-personal interaction among ingroups or hierarchical groups.

Koreans tend to be impolite or even rude when they interact with outgroups like outsiders or strangers. Everyone outside the ingroup is likely to be treated with curiosity or caution or even a bit of suspicion. I still remember that I apologized to an American couple for their having had a hard time trying to get away from the mob surrounding them when they went out shopping.

A few days ago I was waiting for a taxi, standing in a queue. The man just before me shouted at his friend (who had just come to take a taxi) and made his friend stand before him without the slightest regard for those who were eagerly waiting for their turn. This man was very kind to his friend but very impolite to others. This same man might possibly turn out to be very rude when he pushes aside without any compunction someone (who had waited longer than he) and takes a taxi to his home.

During my stay in the United States, I was really struck with the way so many different groups from the world over get along well with each other. I was given the impression that Americans are much more proper than we are in meeting strange people, and it is an admirable part of American life for complete strangers to introduce themselves to each other whenever they meet for the first time. (In Korea, however, it is not proper to go up to a stranger and propose an introduction. In Korea one needs to be introduced to a stranger by a mutual acquaintance.) It seems that Americans' law-abiding spirit and high regard for living in togetherness, social morality and public peace have persisted in majestic continuity from the periods of Greek and Rome, through many centuries to the present day.

Korean people tend to be closer than Americans if they know each other well. Taking friendship for instance, you often see in Korea men and women walking holding hands or arm in arm or even hip to hip with the same sex. It would be a great mistake, however, to think that they have some impure interest in matters of sex. Korean friends often demonstrate their friendship by walking close together with the same sex. Koreans do not avoid bodily contact, whereas Americans think it awkward to stand or walk close to one another. The physically close contacts among Koreans make a foreigner wonder if a wave of homosexuality has permeated Korean society at large. The following excerpt describes the one-sided view of Koreans' human contacts eyed by a foreign visitor (personal communication):

> "When I stepped my first foot into the land of Korea, my first sight of groups of the same sex (men and women) walking hand in hand on the boardwalk confused me to the extent that Confusianism has failed on this land of morning calm. I thought that to live in the city of Seoul would be no more different than to live in San Francisco or New York, two major American cities where a large population of homosexuals harbour around. However, it once again puzzled me, with much surprise this time, when my extended exposure to Korean society made me discover that the scene of these men and women of the same sex walking hand in hand is typical of Korean culture, and reflects nothing but their close friendship."

An American usually has a large number of friends, but only one or two really close friends. One of the things that struck me in the United States is that whereas most men have many acquaintances, few have "friends". They have classmates, business associates, school alumni, playmates on the golf course and companions they drink with, but that is all. Of all the people I have met in America, I know only a few who are close friends. Now when I consider how sociable the Americans are, how amicable and cordial, this is very strange. The only explanation I can give myself is that the pace of American life is so great that few men have time for friendship. Or perhaps it is the sheer size of the nation, since Americans very rarely live their lives in the same city where they grew up. From their college years on, they would be living away from their family, since their job may take them to any state or any city of the vast country. As for Koreans, they have a greater chance of living in the same area where they grew up and where they can easily fall back on their childhood or school friends.

Koreans have few friends in general, but most of them tend to be very close ones. Lee O-Young (1967: 102) quotes from Marshall R. Pihl's comment on the Korean "친구" (friend): The Korean word "friend" has a different concept from the word friend in English. The meaning of friend in Korea is a close friend, whereas in American when you say "friend" it means only someone you know. In Korea you don't call someone a friend unless you know him well. I suppose this kind of notion about friend has given rise to the factionalism, by which Korea has been so deeply plagued.

When Korean friends are doing something, there is more emphasis on who you know or on whose friend you are than on what you are doing. Koreans are often blamed for showing special favor toward the people they know or think as friends or school alumni. They often make sacrifices for their friends to such an extent that they are confused about public and private matters. They tend to fail to make the same distinct cleavage between personal and public funds entrusted to their care.

Many Koreans expect to use their friendships and connections for personal advantages. When they ask for a favor (buthak handa, 부탁한다, it implies that their friends should tackle the problem regardless of reason or common sense. They expect the difficulty to be solved by their friends' "alpha" effort. In a similar situation, American friends would say flatly "no." American instinct does not allow itself to do what goes against logic, reason or common sense. Most of the problems involved in American and Korean cultures have come not with acquaintances, but with too much expectation from friendship. Korean friends become insulted if you do not want to do what they expect you to do. To Koreans, the American appears cold and unfriendly, while the American finds the Korean idea of total friendship stifling. This tells eloquently how different the sociocultural backgrounds of the two countries are. The structure of American culture is based upon social contracts, while personal and emotional relationship underlies the structure of Korean culture.

Here is one story which evidences how badly betrayed a Korean often feels, when an American friend says flatly "no." Some years ago, one American university put up a search for the professor position of Linguistics for which a Korean professor (already teaching in the department) applied as an insider. Since he was the one who founded the program with much devotion for five years and, as a result, the department enjoyed increased enrollment, he was optimistic in obtaining that post, and every body in the department believed that he would be the right person to be chosen for the advertised position. However, his irresistable inquisitiveness to know about the outcome prompted him to ask an American professor in the search committee chosen from the department — the friend whom he got closely acquainted with after his arrival in the department. They were, in fact, close enough to invite each other's family for dinner and at times watched a baseball game with their family at the local stadium. Since the Korean professor honestly believed in his friendship, he couldn't help asking him at what stage the search process had arrived at, while they walked toward the department after one meeting. His American friend responded, "Tom (the Korean's first name), I am sorry that I am not supposed to tell you anything concerning the search process." At hearing this, the Korean professor clenched his upper teeth into the lip of the lower, which reflected his dismay and sense of being betrayed. After this flat rejection from his friend whose friendship he honestly believed in, their friendship turned sour. Since then, the Korean professor turned a cold shoulder to his American friend. At a later point, he asked a Japanese faculty member the same question and with no difficulties obtained all the information he wanted. The Japanese faculty told the Korean professor that she was providing the information as a favor, because she thought that they were colleagues in the department. Moreover, she suggested him to keep this information secret between themselves. It is easy to see that Japanese culture is in tandem with Korean culture, which allowed her to help the Korean colleague by providing the information he badly needed.

Personal relationships are an extremely important consideration in the mind of the Korean people. When face is involved, there is a strong sense of personal responsibility and integrity in whatever they do. Paul S. Crane (1967: 188) says that "where clear-cut responsibility and personal relationships are not delineated, then there is little sense of responsibility. There is little feeling for looking after a public place of the community." Some men may be observed taking care of their bodily functions in the nook of a public place or some another man's house or building but they never relieve themselves in the corner of their own houses. Urine frequently discharged by the drunkards in the evening stunts the growth of the pine trees in front of my house.

While Koreans tend to have extreme impartiality for what belongs either to them or their own groups, they tend to have an utter indifference and even disregard for what belongs to others. Excessive love for ingroups might be considered to be a manifestation of selfishness. Every human relationship is based upon too many personal and emotional things.

Either inside or outside the ingroups, the proper relationships are well maintained vertically-elder-younger, higher-lower in rank. Nobody wants to challenge that hierarchy. The bad thing about Korean society is that it is divided by so many "emotional groups" (e.g. relatives, alumni, close friends, religious groups, academic groups, etc.) that there are too many insurmountable barriers existing in the mind of the Korean people. This is the chief reason why interpersonal communication cannot be successfully carried on horizontally in Korean society. As many opposing groups as there are, there are as many barriers in the human mind.

Even among the people attached to the same ingroup, they tend to keep aloof from each other because of age and sex. Take a Korean family for instance. In daily life the family members live separately from each other. They seldom get together to enjoy each other's company. After a day's work, the father goes out for drinking with his friends. The grandfather does what he wants and spends his time playing cards or "Changgi" (oriental chess, 장기) with his friends at the "Bokdokbang" (real estate office, 복덕방). Brothers and sisters go their separate ways and have a good time with their friends. The mother also goes out for "Kye" (契: 계), a mutual financing association to collect money for her mutual investment group for profit of the investors) and enjoys chatting with her friends. Even when they sit together at meal time, they seldom talk. The father looks at the "nunchi" (눈치) of the grandfather and the children look at the "nunchi" of the father. They eat solemnly and quietly, and chew away as if they were annoyed. They seem to be afraid of having a good time, talking with each other. The atmosphere is almost stultifying. Although a Korean society is family-centered, the Koreans do not really enjoy getting together with their family members. On this Lee O-Young (1967: 107) makes some remarks: Our society is not one built family by family, but rather Korean society is constructed by each family member escaping from the family in his own way according to his age and sex.

2.10. PSYCHO-SOCIOLOGICAL IMPLICATIONS
— THOUGHT PATTERNS AND COMMUNICATION
STYLES —

The thought patterns and mental attitudes underlying Korean linguistic behavior present a considerable problem to cross-cultural
communication. "To suffer a loss" in English is "to see a loss" in
Korean. The Korean speaker of English is likely to be in danger of
using "to see a loss" instead of using "to suffer a loss." Koreans call
the back teeth of the mouth "the love teeth", while to Americans
they are "wisdom teeth," and the English equivalent of the Korean
phrase "the ear of a needle," is "the eye of a needle" (Chang
1911:42). A native speaker of English might say to his customer,
"What can I do for you, sir?" For the same expression a Korean
would say, "What are you looking for, sir?" Koreans often say, "I am
sorry" in the context where an English speaker would say, "Thank

you." Koreans say, "Take great pains (수고하십시오)" in the situation where an English speaker would say, "Good-bye" or "See you again." Misunderstanding often arises when a Korean says, "I know," in a situation where an English speaker says, "I see." About this different use of "I know" and "I see," Lee O-Young (1967: 42-3) gives us an illuminating explanation in his essay "A Culture of the Ear and A Culture of the Eye":

> Western languages are developed on logical aspects, while it has often been indicated that our language is developed in terms of emotion. When we give names to things, we often use an aural image... When we see the (Chinese) word for "light rain" (細雨), we think of it aurally and distinguish between a light drizzle, "posulpi" (보슬비), and a slightly heavier drizzle, "pusulpi" (부슬비)... We do distinguish the aural aspects of Korean with a delicacy of degree difficult to find in foreign languages. For example, when a number of people lie sleeping in the same room, we try to think of different words to describe their breathing. A suckling babe breathes "saeksaek" (색색), a kindergarden schoolchild "k'olk'ol" (콜콜) and a father and mother "k'ulk'ul." (쿨쿨)... In English, when they want to say "I know," they say "I see"; they are people who live mainly by sight. But we say "obey!" (lit. hear my words well), "he doesn't obey" (lit. he doesnt' hear my words well) and "he didn't understand" (lit. the ear is dark). It seems that we understand things by hearing and not by seeing. We also say of a machine which does or doesn't work well that it has no ears (lit. it hears well or it doesn't hear)... Then what in the world is the real difference between seeing and hearing? Professor Park Chong-hong of Seoul National University indicated in his thesis "On Seeing and Hearing" that seeing is "logos" and hearing is "pathos." Thus, so to speak, a culture of the eye is intellectual, rational, theoretical and active, while a culture of the ear is emotional, sensitive, intuitive and passive.

Koreans use "yes" in a linguistic context where Americans say "no." For instance, when a Korean speaker is asked, "Didn't you go to school yesterday?" he will invariably answer, "Yes, I didn't." In English "no" merely indicates the first suggestion of the answer which follows, but in Korean the content of a sentence is not determined at the beginning, but at the end of the sentence. The first response "yes" in this sentence indicates agreement with the inquirer's presupposition that the respondent did not go to school. This kind of mental attitude seems to have originated from the fact that Korean speakers avoid the stimulus which may disturb the other, such as hearing "no" in the beginning of the sentence. In other words, even though the answer is negative, the listener will be embarrassed if the speaker uses a direct "no."[1]

In many aspects of Korean interpersonal communication, one must always take into account the other person's feelings and speak to avoid hurting his feelings. Take a drinking party in Korea for instance. It is the Korean custom to exchange glasses between guests as a token of good will and friendship. If anyone of the guests refuses an offer of a glass with "no," he will ruin the genial atmosphere of the party. Even if he is a non-alcoholic drinker, common courtesy demands that he make some efforts to drink or at least drink for the good of his friends unless he is terribly ill. A flat "no" during such a social interaction is considered very bad form, and will cause damage to the feelings of others. A social interactor born in Korean society gradually learns how to say "no" or refuse with finesse without causing offense.

Koreans, instead of making negative responses like "no," or "I disagree with you," or "I cannot do it," like to use more frequently than Americans "circumlocutory" expressions, such as, "I personally want to do it"; "If I had something"; "I agree with you in principle"; or "I sympathize with you." The avoidance of bold and open negative expressions can be attributed to the fear that it might break up the harmony of the group or it might hurt the feelings of others. It is a kind of ritual which counts in the maintenance of harmony in human relationships. This unconscious avoidance of a direct "no"

---

1. The same kind of truth can be applicable to Orientals like the Japanese. See Keiko Ueda, "Sixteen Ways to Avoid Saying "No" in Japan: A Survey of the Function and Frequency of Japanese Patterns of Declining Requests." The paper was presented at the Conference on Communication Acro. Cultures: Contact and Conflict. I.C.U., Tokyo July 9-17, 1972.

which is determined situationally can be explained as an example of one aspect of "psycho-cultural orientation," which strongly influences the process of interpersonal communication in Korean society.

Even if a Korean speaker gives an answer "yes," this does not always mean a positive answer but simply means, "I fully understand the situation you are in now; go on with your talking." A Korean answer "yes" does not necessarily mean agreement or intention of complying. Misunderstandings may frequently arise if one takes Koreans' "yes" as their consent.

In interpersonal communication, a Korean is careful in his conduct to show the proper respect and concern for the feelings and sensitivities of others. One of the most important factors in influencing conduct and relations with others is the typical Korean word (기분, "kibun"), the word with its cultural overtones and implications. For this rich word, we cannot find a true English equivalent. Paul S. Crane (1967: 7) puts the word "kibun" this way:

> Perhaps the most important thing to an individual Korean is recognition of his "selfhood." The state of his inner feelings, his prestige, his awareness of being recognized as a person, the deference he receives from his fellows — all these factors determine his morale, his face, or self-esteem, essentially his state of mind, which may be expressed in Korean by the word "kibun" (기분 : 氣分)... When the "kibun" is good, one "feels like a million dollars," when bad, one feels like eating worms."

A wise man is quick to see another man's "kibun." This emphasis on mood (the feeling of the moment) and atmosphere is quite in excess of what is considered average in an American culture.

This kind of "affective communication style" (emphasis upon the feelings of the listeners) too often brings about cross-cultural miscommnunication. I still remember reading in an editorial which appeared in the Honolulu Star Bulletin, September, 1972 that there arose a horrible case of miscommunication between the U.S. President and the Japanese Prime Minister in the U.S.-Japan Economic-Trade meeting:

A statement by the Japanese that they understood America's situation was changed in translation to an expression of sympathy for the U.S. position, a quite important difference under the circumstances.

One version of the U.S.-Japan rift over textiles is that it was heightened by a misunderstanding between Prime Minister Sato and President Nixon in their private talk last year. The President thought he received a commitment, but the Prime Minister didn't feel he had made one.

The problems between America and Japan would be serious enough even if we both spoke the same language.

Immediately after the meetings (The U.S.-Japan Economic Trade meetings were held in Washington in September, 1971.), the American government made a thorough analysis of the degree of understanding achieved by each party, and shockingly it was found out that "even with the utilization of capable interpreters, the U.S. delegates understood approximately thirty percent of what the Japanese delegates meant to convey, whereas the Japanese comprehended about thirty five percent of the communication of the U.S. delegates" (Takeyama 1972: 32). Muneo Yoshikawa, a professor of The University of Hawaii, ascribed the cause of miscommunication to the failure of a thorough grasp of the meanings of the silent cultural assumptions which are manifested in the modes of communication patterns.[1] As an example, Yoshikawa takes up "wakarimasu" (to understand) which was misunderstood by the American delegates. The expression "wakarimasu" in Japanese culture, he says, can be interpreted variously depending on the situations. According to him, the Japanese speaker may use the expression to show his sympathy with the listener's position, although he does not necessarily agree

---

1. Prof. Yoshikawa made a presentations on the paper entitled "Psycho-sociological Implications of the Japanese Interpersonal Communication Patterns" in the Third Summer Program in East-West Intercultural Studies(July 21-August 11, 1964) in which the author participated. I am greatly indebted to him for this section.

with the listener's view. Yoshikawa uses another example which reads like this: "Jijoo wa yoku wakarimashita. Dekirudake zenshosuruyoo tsutomete-mimashoo," which may be translated as," I fully understand the circumstances or position you are in, and I' ll do my best." This kind of expression may be taken by American listeners as a kind of agreement or commitment.

This kind of statement in Japanese culture is often a polite way of saying, "I cannot do it" (Takeyama 1972: 32). Another example illustrated by Yoshikawa is : "Watakushi kojin to shite wa, mattaku dookan desu," which may be roughly translated as "I personally feel exactly the same as you do." The key term which is likely to cause misunderstanding is "kojin" which means "personal" or "individual." The underlying implication of this term is: "I agree with you in principle, but being a member of the group, I alone cannot do anything about it" (Yoshikawa 1974: 4). (The probability is that the Japanese Prime Minister is not given so much power as the U.S. President in the decision-making mechanism.) What should be noted here however, as Yoshikawa points out, is the fact that it was recorded in the official paper from the White House that at the Summit Conference of 1969, Prime Minister Sato promised President Nixon that he would come up with a solution to the pressing textile problem by the end of 1969. The President thought he received a commitment, but the Prime Minister did not feel he had made one.

These kinds of interpersonal communication patterns commonly used by Oriental peoples like Koreans or Japanese can be aptly termed a "situation-oriented pattern," the philosophy of which is based upon the idea that it is better to be harmonious than right or sincere. Regarding the concept of harmony, Walsh (1973: 82) writes:

> One of the basic differences between Eastern and Western cultures is that the Eastern are dominated by the concept of harmony; the Western by power. In the East, it is said, knowledge is for the sake of living in better and closer harmony with nature and man; in the West, knowledge is for the sake of controlling peace and order is a prime value; in the West, achieving the things that power makes possible is considered by many as a primary goal.

For the sake of living in harmony with each other, Orientals like Koreans or Japanese tend to do everything to avoid appearing to oppose anyone directly. This pattern places emphasis upon the feelings of others, whereas Americans tend to draw heavily on the language itself to convey without understanding the silent assumptions of Korean or Japanese culture. These American patterns which place emphasis on getting the message across can be aptly called as the "instrumental" communication style. In this communication pattern, verbally expressed messages play an important role, whereas in an "affective" or "situation-oriented" communication style like that of the Koreans or Japanese, non-linguistic elements such as feelings and attitudes play an important role in the interpersonal communication. This is another way of saying that the instrumental communication style places the emphasis of communication on ideas or thoughts, and the affective communication style emphasizes the communication of feelings.

In connection with this, there is "nunchi" (눈치), a kind of sense by which Koreans can detect whether others are really pleased and satisfied or not. Kim (1975: 7) and Steinberg explain about "nunchi" which is literally translated as "eye-measure" :

> "Nunchi" is a kind of "sense", but it cannot simply be explained as "sense." "Nunchi" is an interpretation of others' facial expressions or what they say plus a mysterious "alpha" hidden in their inner hearts. "Nunchi" is usually an interpretation by the lower social class of the feelings of the higher social class, necessary in an unreasonable society in which logic and inflexible rules have no place. Americans do not compromise or concede when it is contrary to common sense, regardless of the rank of the other person. But in our case, if we try to explain something to a superior on the basis of common sense, this is regarded as impertinent and reproachable. Therefore, there is no other way but to solve problems with "nunchi" detecting the other person's facial expression plus "alpha" hidden in his inner heart.

It must be noted here that there is a striking contrast in American and Korean attitudes toward verbal language. In an instrumental communication pattern, like that of the Americans, people assert themselves or make themselves understood by talking, (this can be called a "self-assertive communication style), whereas in a situation communication style like that of Koreans or Japanese, people try to defend themselves either by vague expressions or by not talking. Americans try to persuade their listeners in the step-by-step process whether or not their listeners accept them totally. But a Korean or a Japanese tends to refuse to talk any further in the course of a conversation with someone once he decides that he cannot accept the other's attitude, his way of thinking and feeling in totality. This kind of attitude often leads to either "total understanding" or "no understanding at all" (Yoshikawa 1974: 11). This is what makes such a wide gap between the American style of partial communication and the Korean or Japanese style of total communication.

When Koreans do some kinds of business transactions, they approach the persons they want to meet by way of an introduction through their friends. Once a human relationship is established, they convey their messages through the channel of food or drink. This type of Korean communication pattern can be characterized as an indirect-intermediated interpersonal communication pattern. In Korea a language itself plays a less central role: it is a part of a larger system of "cultural" means of communication. In contrast, Americans tend to solve problems through the direct face-to-face interpersonal communication pattern, which is motivated by a self-assertive oriented attitude. Americans put sincerity and directness before harmony in interpersonal communication patterns.

The cultural trait that Koreans exercise "Nunchi" or "Indirect Talking" in their daily communication is often perceived as a factor of disgrace or dishonesty to some foreigners. They do not understand why verbal communications among Koreans are subject to reliance on something that is not reliable and subjective. They charge that the imprecise nature of communication based on "Nunchi" or "Indirect Talking" often leads to miscommunication and thus decreases the effectiveness of oral communication. Moreover, they make a point that when one does not base one's communication on the explicit verbal message and instead beats around the bush, one is intentionally misleading the listener, and is then at the brink of being dishonest and even sneaky. As a consequence, foreigners naive to the ways in which Koreans communicate among themselves tend to downplay this cultural trait to the point where one should not trust Koreans. This somewhat harsh criticism by Americans does not make their own culture defenseless either. Many Koreans have a low opinion of Americans appealing to a self-assertive communication style. When Koreans are engaged in verbal communication with Americans, one of the difficulties they are immediately faced with is the situation where they are empowered to make an explicit "yes or no" answer to the transmitted message in a flow of information, regardles of whether one answer over the other will save them or put them into a trouble. Since their cultural orientation conditions them to apply a time lag to making a certain kind of decision, so as not to make any possible mistakes(which they might have to correct at a later point), they want to be more cautious and careful before sending out the message. This precarious attitude of Koreans delays their response and sometimes gets the communication out of rhythm. However, in the process they less frequently run into a situation where they have to say, "I am sorry. I made a mistake, or I changed my mind (which Amricans very often do)."

The Korean daily conversation style can be characterized as a "prose-oriented communication pattern." Instead of going directly to the point, Koreans tend to take up long descriptive accounts about a person or an event in subjective terms. This is the dialogue between a Korean immigrant and an American employer during an interview, which actually happened in San Francisco (I obtained the material from the Korean-English Language & Job Training Program in San Francisco):

Employer: Are you confident in performing the duties of a file clerk?
Korean: Yes, I am. I have a B.A. degree from Seoul University. My family is known to be good one, and I have been getting whatever I want from everybody.

Employer: But, have you ever worked in a filing department in any company?
Korean: Yes, I can. I can type, drive, and have a B.A. degree from the best
           university in Korea.
Employer: Can you order things alphabetically?
Korean: I learned English for six years in high school and four years at
           college. I used to be the best student in those days.

This kind of prose-oriented communication pattern, encouraging Koreans not to answer questions directly, would be intolerable to Americans. Americans who listen to this kind of conversation feel for sure that it lacks substance or significance.

This style of conversation is not dialectically oriented. No data and evidence are usually given to prove the point one wants to make. The essence of pleasure in conversation, for Koreans, is not in discussion as a game of logic but in emotional exchange. For this reason, debates among Korean people quickly reach high emotional pitch. In fact, calm rational arguments are looked down upon as "a mere language game." This lack of a dialectic style of speech can be attributed to the lack of discipline in relationships between daily interactors. The Koreans have not been trained in going through the three steps of dialectic reasoning.

All these boil down to a single statement: the difference of psychocultural orientation patterns between two cultures is what actually happens in the process of communication between the affective communication-oriented people and the instrumental communication oriented people; the situation-oriented people and the self-assertive-oriented people; the total communication-oriented people and the partial communication-oriented people; the indirect-intermediated interpersonal communication-oriented people and direct face-to-face oriented people; the non-dialectic-oriented people and the dialectic oriented people (cf. Yoshikawa: 1974).

Just as each culture has its own language, so does it also have its own logic. Cross-cultural communication can not be carried on successfully unless this logic is understood. Logic must be understood fully before the culture can be understood. Every cross-cultural communicator tends to interpret another culture in terms of his own logic or that with which he is most familiar. Orientals like Koreans or Japanese tend to bring to the study of Western culture their own logic based on Buddhism or Confucianism. I once heard that a Korean student studying Milton in an American university had been frequently cautioned against his deeply rooted oriental way of logic by his academic advisor.

Anyone who has been long exposed to oriental cultures in which Buddhism had had a dominating influence knows that it has three cornerstones. They are: "Anisa", "Dukkha," and "Anata." "Anisa" means that everything determinate is changing. "Dukkha," means that life in this world is full of suffering. "Anata" means that there is no determinate self. These three philosophical ideas are accepted by all Buddhists, regardless of the particular philosophical school to which they belong (Win 1964: 225-8).

To attempt to understand Christianity or either traditional Aristotelian or modern symbolic logic, using Buddhism, is bound to miss the point. In the thoughts and attitudes of Korean Christians, they are in reality much more Buddhistic or Confucian than Christian.

For an Easterner to read the Bible or Aristotle or Plato or Milton, for example, or for a Westerner to read Buddhism or Confucianism or the Upanishads or the Bhagavadgita is a big step toward a successful cross-cultural communication. In most cases, a person takes a new view of his own logic or cultural values after studying those of another. Every person understands his own culture better through realizing how the two different logics interact.

Last but not least, to accomplish successful cross-cultural communication, there must be a change in the negative attitudes of the people of one culture toward those of another. Continuous efforts to better understand another culture will help reinforce positive attitudes. Attitudes are based in part on knowledge and in part on feelings. By showing a willingness to approach something, attitudes based on accurate and genuine knowledge will encourage cross-cultural communication, whereas attitudes based on feelings, which indicate a desire to avoid something, will stand in the way of arriving at genuine knowledge and discourage successful communication. Very often, attitudes or feelings, such as superiorty-inferiority, hatred, distrust, resentment and jealousy might prevent successful cross-cultural communication.

In addition to contrasting communication patterns and styles between Koreans and Americans, the Korean inferiority complex toward Americans, though often not recognized at their conscious level, could prevent smooth relationships. In fact, the American-Korean relationship has been a kind of master-follower relationship. It has been a "one way communication." So long as Koreans look upon Americans as their "big brothers," cross-cultural communication can go on without much trouble. But the unilateral withdrawal of American troops from Korea might change the situation. Likewise, the Japanese superiority complex toward Southeast Asians, as Yoshikawa warns, may hinder communication with them. Obviously, a superiority complex on the part of Americans, along with the withdrawal of American troops from Korea might come into direct conflict with the "nationalism" of the Korean people or presumably the Japanese people, whereas the Japanese superiority complex might come in direct conflict with the "nationalism" of the Southeast Asian people.

In most cases, negative attitudes are irrational, the result of preconceptions or prejudices. One of the intrinsic goals of cross-cultural communication is to avoid making premature judgments about other peoples. Cross-cultural communication should be carried on on the individual merits, on the evidence, rather than on vague impressions or prejudices. Heart-to-heart communication implies an openness and willingness on both sides to change attitudes. Assuming that there will be some antagonisms, sharply divergent opinions, or justified anger in cross-cultural communication, we should make every effort to work out these differences rationally and in a friendly manner rather than emotionally and destructively.

Chapter 3

UNDERLYING HUMAN SIMILARITY

Perhaps because differences are more obvious and recognizable, the average layman in viewing a foreign culture tends to notice the differences more than the similarities. It must not be overlooked, however, that there is quite a number of similar patterns of behavior in different cultures. Take the following for instance. We can accurately or reliably identify the emotion shown on a person's face. When a person becomes angry, no matter where he lives in the world, the universal characteristic is that his brows are usually lowered, the muscles around his eyes become tense, and his lips are tightly pressed together. There is definitely a relationship between what a person is feeling, what he can show on his face, and what people think he is feeling. But the way people control their facial expressions differs from culture to culture.

A number of recent studies in cross-cultural psychology have shown that the facial expressions of emotion are universally the same. When a person is feeling angry or sad or happy and is making no attempt to camouflage his feelings, he has the same facial expressions whether he lives in Korea, the United States, Japan or South Africa. Basic emotions are built into the individual, but one learns stimuli for triggering a specific emotion, and one learns how to modify the resulting behavior. Thus all people, be they Koreans or Americans, share the neurophysiological elements corresponding to fear, disgust, anger or happiness, but they can learn what to be angry about for example, and they can learn how and when to manage their corresponding behavior when the emotion is experienced.

Every culture has some specific stimuli caused by certain things or events. Take the sound of a siren in Seoul. It has a quite different effect upon Koreans who live under the constant fear of sudden attack by North Korea, as opposed to a person who lives in the United States. As another example suggested by Jerry D. Boucher,[1] most Koreans consider dogs and cats as fierce and unclean and thus they are filled with disgust and fear by their approach. Most Americans, on the other hand, regard dogs and cats as man's best friends. Dr. Boucher says regarding specific stimuli such as sirens and dogs and cats that rather than referring to sirens and dogs as the causes of emotion, it might be more correct to label the stimuli of those events as something dangerous and unclean, and perhaps disgust and fear are universal responses to the class of stimuli labeled "unclean" or "dangerous."

Every culture has "display rules" and develops them about how, when and where a person can or cannot display his feelings. As illustrated, there is a "display rule" in Korean culture that respect for elders should be taken for granted, and people should not express affectionate behavior or gestures in the presence of others. Public display of affection is ridiculous and even scorned sometimes in Korea. American couples smile and even kiss at their weddings, looking happy, but in a Korean situation neither the bride nor the bridegroom is supposed to smile. They should look serious throughout their wedding ceremony. Whoever shows enthusiasm and affection in public is regarded as light-hearted or even frivolous. But it is not difficult to imagine that they are wearing a happy smile when left alone in their private room. As another example quoted from Boucher's article, "a rather curious set of rules seems to govern displays of emotion at beauty contests in America: the winner (who is presumably happy) should cry, while the losers (who are presumably

---

1. I am greatly indebted to Dr. Jerry D. Boucher's article appearing in Newsletter, Culture and Language Learning, East-West Center, pp. 2-4 (March 1,1974) and to his lecture conducted in The Third Summer Program in East-West Intercultural Studies (July 21-August 11, 1974) where the author participated. Dr. Boucher coordinated the seminar. He is one of the most noted specialists in emotional behavior and cross-cultural psychology.

sad) are supposed to smile, or even further, show great delight towards the winner." But it is not hard, as Boucher predicts, to surmise that, in the privacy of their hotel rooms one would see a smiling winner and rather glum losers.

"Going Dutch" in America and "eating together and not paying separately" in Korea are not basically too different. Eating together and paying for someone else in Korea is not a repeatedly practiced one sided game. One person pays for his friend today and his friend in turn will pay for him tomorrow. The display rule in America is that they eat together and pay separately, whereas the display rule in Korea is that they eat together and take turns paying for someone else.

Although languages display superficial differences in phonology, grammar, and semantics which make them mutually unintelligible, recent comparative studies in linguistics show that at a deeper level languages display certain universals which make them translatable. Many researchers in anthropology, linguistics, sociology, psychology, and other fields seek to test the hypothesis that regardless of language or culture, human beings use the same qualifying (descriptive) framework in allocating the affective meanings of concepts (involving values, attitudes, feelings, etc.). They are seeking a framework of common affective components that is constant across the human species, and the primary hypothesis about affective semantic universality has been verified. Charles E. Osgood (1975) has been concerned with semantic similarities across human cultures and languages, and has found evidence for similarities at all levels. In his *Cross-Cultural Universals of Affective Meaning*, Osgood deals with underlying similarities or universals across language/culture communities. Human beings, no matter where they live or what language they speak, apparently abstract about the same properties of things for making comparisons (e.g. large, big-small, little, good-bad, young-old, thin-thick, black-white, strong-weak, fast-slow, hard-soft, tall-short, etc.), and they order these different modes of qualifying in roughly the same way in importance.

This "universalist" point of view was recently bolstered by the school of Chomskyans who claimed that language is basically innate, or genetically inherited capability, which all human beings are programmed from birth to develop. They argue that there is a universal set of semantic categories from which each language draws its own subset of categories, which makes languages differ on the surface level. A classical example of this view is Berlin and Kay (1969)' s research on color categories that seem different among the world' s languages. The basic tenet of their hypothesis is that there is an exact set of eleven color terms, which may or may not be present in a given language:

white		green			purple
	⟨ red ⟨		⟨ blue ⟨	brown ⟨	pink
					orange
black		yellow			grey

But interesting to this hypothesis is that these terms are ordered in a certain way, as shown above by the symbol. Thus, if a language has the colors "green and yellow," then it must also contain other colors (e.g., white, black, and red) which precede these two colors in the above ordered relation. Another example of the 'universalist' trend is kinship terminology which offers the fascination of a relatively homogeneous set of lexical meanings whose organization differs markedly from language to language, and yet somehow has an underlying element of uniformity (Leech, 1981). Leech envisions that in this case the common ground between languages is cultural rather than perceptual.

Human nature is not fundamentally different. It is only the convention, the form, the incidentals that differ from culture to culture, but the fundamentals of passion, intellect and imagination go beyond the cultural boundaries. Conventions and traditions, prejudices and ideals and religious beliefs, moral systems and codes of good manners, varying according to the geographical and historical circum-stances, mould into different forms the unchanging material of human instinct, passion, and desire.

The hardly ambitious intent of this book is to illustrate by my per-sonal experiences some of the more apparent cross-cultural dispari-ties between Korea and the United States. As vital to my interest in cross-cultural studies as this task is, however, the underlying human similarity between the cultures is apparent. The human experience has presented both cultures with the same, social stimuli demanding some articulation of behavior. Oceans and epochs have influenced the unique differentiation of that articulation that my observations hopefully evidenced. One can make no value judgments regarding the suitability of either society's cultural conclusions. It is enough indeed to look and wonder.

3.1. A UNIVERSAL CULTURE

Although there is ample evidence that men are becoming more nationalistic and ethnocentric now than ever before, there is none the less a strong tendency for the world to move toward a universal culture. A man's sense of belonging to one world has never been keener than at present. Some great men, like Gandhi in the past, had faith that the world is one in its deepest roots and highest aspirations. They knew that the purpose of historical humanity was to develop a world civilization, a world-culture, a world community.

The nature of the world and of man's relation to it and to his fellows has changed radically with the growth of new forms of communication and transportation, and with the increase in scientific and technical knowledge and modernization generally. Man's outlook had to change with it, since scientific and technical knowledge is the same for all men everywhere regardless of culture and regardless of how they adapt it and use it. A world or universal culture is now not only possible, it is also imperative for both human progress and survival (Walsh 1973: 86). Yet the emphasis today on this evident fact itself implies that while every individual is affected by the quickening flow of world events, he is still strongly influenced by the ways of living and thinking in his own nation and culture (Nakamura 1969: 3).

A universal culture does not mean a call for the eventual disappearance of all individual cultures, or their amalgamation into some uniform culture, but a call for the emergence of a universal or human culture which has a profound respect for individual cultures. Each culture contributes something vital and unique to a world culture. A universal culture draws together those universal ideas and values that all men share. Korea, for example, instead of thinking of cutting herself off from the world community by seeking isolationism, can vigorously participate in that community in her own distinctive way, and contribute something of her spirit to it.

A universal culture does not imply that one of the existing cultures would win universal acceptance. It never involves any one culture's forcing itself on others in any form of cultural imperialism. It also does not mean uniformity. A culture can be universal without being uniform or so standardized that all cultural differences disappear.

Every culture should be competitive to contribute its creative intelligence to the universal culture. The clash of ideas leads to new and better ideas. A culture is like an individual; unless it is competing for something, it stagnates and too readily settles for things as they are. Out of competition comes greater initiative, sharper thinking and clarification of issues, and new inventions.

Then what are the factors that make universal culture possible? It is through knowing human similarities rather than differences that one realizes that man is already on the way to a universal culture. Human similarities arise from two principal sources: first, that man, wherever he lives in the world, has a body as well as a mind, and second, that he has an intelligence and reason, and is a philosophizing animal.

Biologically, a human being has similar needs for clothing, food, shelter, and procreation, and each culture has organized ways of furnishing these basic necessities. Not only are the needs themselves similar, but also the ways of satisfying them are also quite similar. The methods of agriculture, for example, may differ in the degree of efficiency from culture to culture, but they all include the same fundamental processes, viz. cultivating, sowing, harvesting, and it is only natural that a man everywhere finds similar, though not necessarily identical, ways of conducting these processes. There is also remarkable similarity in the ways in which different cultures handle and procure food. Men everywhere usually take three meals a day and perform their bodily functions regularly and continue to produce offspring.

Man is not only a biological species; he is a special and unique case in that he is also directed by reason and intelligence. Man has been called Homo Sapiens "because he is intelligent, capable not merely of instinct and sense experience but also of conceptualization, of imagination and creativity, and of problem solving." Different people, of course, have different degrees of intelligence and they use their intelligence differently; but man living, man at work or at play, is an intelligent being (Walsh 1973: 88). Since intelligence and reason are not confined to a particular culture, they are universal phenomena.

Mistakes and erroneous judgments result from incorrect or insufficient knowledge or faulty reasoning, but these are sometimes due to the lack of training rather than of reason or intelligence. The simple fact is that human intelligence is generally limited in its nature and potentiality. For this reason, some people stress the necessity of the training of human intelligence to develop a world culture. They argue that misunderstanding and conflict do not arise out of intelligence and reason but out of emotion. Their opinion is that a world culture would be relatively easy, if men everywhere were strictly rational and reasonable, and if they defined intelligence, rationality, and reasonableness in the same way.

But there are "vast dark areas of the individual and the collective subconscious, including likes and dislikes, loves and fears, which go into the shaping of man's thoughts and actions and of which he is not always aware" (Walsh 1973: 88). Hence there is the room for training human intelligence. The man whose intelligence has not been trained tends to depend heavily on emotion and feeling; "his reactions tend to be instinctive, compulsive, and sometimes aggressive; natural rather than cultivated or civilized." Emotions are, indeed, an important part of human life, which we can not deny or underestimate, but the effort must be constantly made to bring the emotions more and more under the control of reason.

Once man has provided for his basic biological necessities, he begins to philosophize. He turns to "the questions of how to interpret himself, his fellow men, his world and nature's, and of how to organize his life so that he can find the greatest possible realization and happiness as a human." The philosophizing process is universal and similar in all cultures. The premises or starting points, however, are different from culture to culture, and consequently the conclusions become dissimilar. The reason that people of various culture start from different premises in their philosophizing process is that different cultures not only have different histories, experiences, problems, and religious and philosophical insights and different interests and purposes that greatly affect their thinking, but also find different premises sufficient to account for the phenomena of life.

What makes up a culture is the very fact that the people in it experience the real world in their own way. The experience each person has is different from that of any other, and different cultures place varying emphasis on differing aspects of their experience. Walsh (1973: 81) remarks, therefore, that the study of a culture includes its psychology, its perceptions of beauty, its regard for people and things, its political and military organization, its cognitive and affective levels, its economic status, and its ethical patterns.

3.2. COMMON HUMAN NATURE AND SAME LOGIC

All men have a common human nature. What is held most true and valuable involved in the scale of real goods that constitute a good human life is relative only to human nature, not to societies or cultures. It provides a standard that transcends the mores and the diverse value-systems that are inherent in diverse cultures. It is universally applicable because it is based on what is universally present in all societies — human beings, the same in their specific natures(Adler 1970: 122-23). An idea is not good merely because it is old nor because it is new. It is not good because it is a Western idea or an Eastern idea, nor because it is ours. Ideas are good because they indicate a correspondence between what is judged to be true and what is in fact true. An emerging universal culture would transcend all presently existing cultures, but would incorporate in some creative way all that the peoples of the various cultures now hold most true and valuable.

A great book goes beyond cultural boundaries. A great book is not great merely because it is good only for a particular people but because it gives an illumination and revelation to every human mind across cultures. What do you think would happen to our modern world without the cultural and spiritual restraint that comes from the growth of the human mind through wisdom absorbed from the great books? A great book of fiction or romance or poetry has not been composed according to the principles of what is true of a nation or a certain period in the history, but according to the best principles of the great science of life, i.e. the knowledge of human nature. The fact that we can still understand the earliest known specimens of art and literature and can recognize in some of them an unsurpassed artistic excellence is proof enough that what human mind holds most dear, true and valuable in the remotest times is precisely what it is now.

Although there are dozens or even hundreds of subcultures within the broad Eastern and Western cultures, a number of theorists conclude that the basic differences in the actions and behavior patterns that flow from the ways of human knowing can be boiled down broadly to those of the East and those of the West. Radhakrishnan (1962: 255) even doubts that there are fundamental differences between East and West. He remarks that:

> there is no reason to believe that there are fundamental differences between the East and the West. Human beings are everywhere human and hold the same deepest values. The differences which are, no doubt, significant are related to external, temporary social conditions and are alterable with them. East and West are relative terms. They are geographical expressions and not cultural types.

A similar statement is made by Clyde Kluckhohn (1949: 356):

> There is much more to social and cultural phenomena than immediately meets the ear and eye ⋯ The strain toward consistency which Sumner noted in the folkways and mores of all groups cannot be accounted for unless one postulates a more or less systematic pattern of reaction to expe-

rience as a characteristic property of all integrated cultures. In a certain deep sense the logic (that is, the manner of interpreting relationships between phenomena) of all members of the human species is the same. It is the premises that are different.

In every aspect of life, whether it be transportation facilities, political systems, or even ethical ideas and family relations, it can not be denied that Easterners and Westerners today have much more in common than they did a century ago. There are many signs everywhere in the world of the growth of what may be called a common world culture. Reischauer and Fairbank (1958: 6) in their masterful study *East Asia, The Great Tradition* write:

> Ultimately the growth of this common world culture and of the mutual interest may greatly facilitate harmonious understanding among the various parts of the world.

According to some anthropologists, a universal culture will emerge in a more or less natural evolutionary way. As the peoples of the world draw closer and closer together geographically, so they will psychologically. Whatever differences continue to exist will be minor ones resulting from such things as differences in climate, styles of dress, and eating habits. It is utterly absurd for the people of any culture to hold on to ideas and habits they have come to consider obsolete simply to preserve cultural differences. Ideas that cannot stand up under the pressure of this new world trend toward a universal culture will disappear except in history and anthropology texts. The fittest ideas will survive and become commonly or generally accepted (Walsh 1973: 75).

As pointed out in the beginning paragraphs of this section, a universal culture should not be allowed to take the course of a uniform culture. For a universal culture much will depend on the nature of the struggle of ideas that will take place and the extent of the creative intelligence contributed by each culture. This struggle, instead of involving some kind of cultural domination or imperialism (based on military force or ideological closure) or an exaggerated regard for science and technology, should be a fair and open one. If the people neglect to exercise their own creative intelligence and surrender their own ideas and values and their own integrity in preference to another culture or in the name of modernization, the whole human race might be culturally and spiritually impoverished. What is called for in a universal culture is seeking to preserve the uniqueness of individual cultures while emphasizing the possibility of a worldwide human culture.

Chapter 4

Collected Papers on Cross-Cultural Communication

This chapter includes a collection of Professor Park's seven collaborative articles that he published in the journals of communication in recent years. Donald W. Klopf, a major collaborator, is emeritus professor of West Virginia University and served as former President of the World Communication Association. Other collaborators are Professor Klopf's colleagues at American universities.

Central to the themes of the first five research articles are cultural differences in the behavior of Koreans and Americans, ranging from tactile avoidance, world view, and self-monitoring, human values, and patterns of communicative behavior.

The other two deal with comparing Korean oral communication patterns and communication apprehension with those of Americans, Swiss, and Japanese. One may note that these studies of his make a great departure from the vein of his previous writings in that they are not only experimental in design and statistical analysis, but also well focused on proving specific inquiries under investigation.

The author hopes that the inclusion of these articles will enhance the quality of the present volume, when compared to its predecessor because of its extended coverage of materials in the area of cross-cultural communication.

1. CHARACTERISTICS OF KOREAN ORAL COMMUNICATION PATTERNS*

Myng-Seok Park
Dankook University

Ronald Cambra
University of Hawaii

Donald W. Klopf
West Virginia University

* Korea Journal, Vol.19, No.7, July 1979, Pages 4-8

Observations of Korean speaking habits imply that the typical Korean is out-going, talkative and generally at ease in most oral communication situations. McQuerry contends that Koreans are aggressive, conspicuous and more temperamental than is usually expected of Orientals.[1] Cha, Choi and Suh note that Americans consider Koreans to be relatively active, aggressive, pleasant, industrious, friendly, and fast. An important segment of the population, businessmen, were said to be easy to understand, moving, informative, believable, pleasant, stimulating, friendly and comfortable.[2] Oliver claims that individual expression of opinion characterizes Koreans and this seems to have been fostered by a strong village government system which encouraged free discussion.[3] Klopf, Ishii and Cambra found the Koreans to be less apprehensive about communicating than Americans, Australians and Japanese.[4]

These observations suggest a people who are orally expressive, perhaps, argumentative. Is this the case? Are the Korean orally predisposed? How do they relate interpersonally with others? What satisfactions do they have interacting with others in groups? To answer questions such as these, we have investigated characteristics of Korean speaking in an exploratory fashion. The results of our investigation, along with an explanation of the research methodology and data analysis, are reported here. To make the results more meaningful, we compared the Koreans with groups in three other nations, specifically America, Australia and Japan.

RESEARCH PROCEDURES

To make the comparisons, three instruments were administered in August 1978 to university students in the four countries. The instruments were the Predispositions toward Verbal Behavior (PVB),[5] the Fundamental Interpersonal Relations Orientation-Behavior (FIRO-B)[6] and the Orientation Inventory (Ori).[7] The PVB measures the impressions people hold of the way they orally express themselves to others. The FIRO-B assesses in people the strength of three social needs (inclusion, control and affection) — needs which have the greatest effect on how people relate to each other. The Ori reveals how people interact with others in task-related actvities.

These scales have proven to be reliable and valid, with the validity in each instance based on extensive use. In addition, all have had transcultural application.[8] However, transcultural research presents epistemological and methodological problems that could muddle the results. Hence, we consider this research exploratory and the results tentative.

The students tested were: in Korea, 73 English majors enrolled in Hankuk University of Foreign Studies; in America, 397 University of Hawaii students; in Australia, 219 Armidale College of Advanced Education students; and in Japan, 504 Otsuma Women's, Nihon, Waseda and Yokohama City University students. The students were equally mixed groups of males and females, in an age range of 18 to 24 years, and at a similar educational level. The Koreans and Japanese were English-trained and capable of responding to the three instruments in their English versions. In those countries teachers of English as a second language collaborated in collecting the data.

Tuccy's T-Test Procedure was used in the data analysis. He designed this procedure to calculate the t for independent samples of unequal size — the characteristic of the four groups tested in this research — using computerized programming.[9]

RESULTS

The results are presented next, scale-by-scale, along with an explanation of the behavior each measures.

PVB. People have impressions of their verbal predispositions. These impressions tend to be consistent from one type of speaking situation to another. That is to say, if a person sees himself as speaking slow and deliberate in conversation with another, he sees himself speaking the same way in small groups and as a public speaker. Usually one person's impressions or images of his speaking are confirmed by the impressions others have of his speaking. In fact, the person's impressions may have come originally from the observations others made of his manner of speech.

People's impressions of their verbal behavior come from five aspects of their speaking. These are: (1) dominating communication situations, (2) assuming responsibility for initiating and maintaining interpersonal communication, (3) communicating frequently and at length, (4) being reluctant or disinclined to engage in communication, and (5) being fluent or anxious when communicating. The PVB scale measures the five factors.[10]

PVB COMPARISONS FOR
FIVE COMMUNICATION FACTORS

Group	Mean	Standard Deviation	*t* value
1. Dominance			
Koreans compared to:	31.51	5.47	
a. Americans	23.25	7.00	8.80**
b. Australians	23.50	7.13	8.08**
c. Japanese	25.19	5.85	8.02**
2. Initiating/Maintaining Communication			
Koreans compared to:	28.13	4.88	
a. Americans	29.37	7.41	1.26*
b. Australians	30.74	6.67	2.82***
c. Japanese	29.09	6.48	1.11*
3. Frequency/Duration			
Koreans compared to:	21.10	4.81	
a. Americans	20.94	4.88	23*
b. Australians	21.77	4.38	1.02*
c. Japanese	20.15	4.71	1.48*

4. Disinclination to Communicate			
Koreans compared to:	18.97	4.20	
a. Americans	20.46	4.39	2.49***
b. Australians	21.49	4.52	3.88**
c. Japanese	19.53	4.18	.99*
5. Fluency/Anxiety			
Koreans compared to:	12.05	3.42	
a. Americans	12.58	3.65	1.08*
b. Australians	13.10	3.31	2.14***
c. Japanese	11.90	3.03	.37*

N=Koreans-73; Americans-397; Australians-219; Japanese-504.
*N.S.D.   **p<.001   ***p<.05

Table 1 gives the factor-by-factor comparisons. Compared to the other groups, the Koreans (1) on the dominance factor were significantly different than the others indicating that they are more inclined to dominate in oral encounters; (2) on initiating and maintaining communication they were significantly different than the Australians but not the Americans and Japanese; (3) on frequency and duration they were not significantly different than the others; (4) on disinclination to communicate they were significantly different than the Americans and Australians but not the Japanese; and (5) on fluency and anxiety they were significantly different only than the Australians. These findings lend support to the conclusion that the Koreans are apt to try to dominate oral communication situations and are inclined to be talkative.

FIRO-B. According to many motivational theories, people behave the way they do in order to satisfy certain needs, desires or wants. Some needs can be satisfied only in the company of other people and these needs and interpersonal communication are fundamentally interdependent. Communication is the medium through which these needs are satisfied.

The FIRO-B inventory measures three of these needs-inclusion, control and affection. Inclusion is the desire, or its opposite, a lack of desire, to be accepted, understood and listened to. People join groups and socialize to help satisfy inclusion needs. Control is the desire, or lack of desire, to control others, be in charge, or make decisions. People try to satisfy this need by being orally aggressive and dominant. Affection is the desire, or lack of desire, to have close, personal relations with others. It is seen in the extent to which people will initiate relations or in the capacity to want love.

Two dimensions exist for each need—expressed and wanted. For instance, expressed control is how much a person expresses or tries to give. Wanted control is how much control a person likes to get from others or how much the person wants to receive. The FIRO-B distinguishes between the two dimensions.[12] Table 2 presents the results for the two.

For inclusion, the Table 2 results suggest that the Koreans had satisfied this need much more than the Americans and Australians. In contrast, the Japanese were most satisfied, showing no significant difference with the Koreans on the expressed dimension and a significantly lower score on the wanted dimension.

For control, the Koreans had a stronger need to express control in interpersonal relations than the Americans, Australians and Japanese. In terms of wanted control, the Koreans were no different than the Americans and Japanese. The Australians, on the other hand, had the weakest control need on the wanted dimension, when compared to the Koreans.

For affection, the only significant difference between the Koreans and the other groups appeared when the Japanese and Koreans were compared, with the Japanese having a lower need, being most satisfied.

The FIRO-B findings imply that the Koreans tend to control oral interactions, supporting the PVB results. Their talk, however, will not be directed to satisfying inclusion or affection needs since these needs appear to be well-satisfied. What they are more inclined to talk about is seen in the Ori scale results.

Table 2 FIRO-B COMPARISONS FOR INTERPERSONAL NEEDS ON TWO DIMENSIONS

Group	Mean	Expressed Standard Deviation	*t* value	Mean	Wanted Standard Deviation	*t* value
1. Inclusion						
Korean compared to:	3.97	1.94		2.82	2.69	
a. Americans	4.60	2.20	2.63***	4.77	3.40	4.13**
b. Australians	5.06	2.10	4.07**	5.13	3.27	4.86**
c. Japanese	3.90	1.90	.43**	1.61	2.58	3.36**
2. Control						
Koreans compared to:	4.61	2.40		3.67	1.82	
a. Americans	2.11	2.14	8.13**	3.79	2.49	.37*
b. Australians	1.80	2.08	8.66**	2.91	2.23	2.36***
c. Japanese	1.83	1.90	10.22**	4.09	2.16	1.43*
3. Affection						
Koreans compard to:	4.81	2.48		5.21	2.53	
a. Americans	4.45	2.71	.93*	5.39	2.74	.46*
b. Australians	4.52	2.58	.72*	5.33	2.55	.32*
c. Japanese	4.83	2.54	.09*	4.36	2.23	2.70***

N=Koreans-73; Americans-397; Australians-219; Japanese-504.
*N.S.D.   **p<.001   ***p<.05

Ori. How a person reacts to the challenge of a group task and to those interacting with him depends upon the kinds of satisfactions and rewards he seeks and the dissatisfactions most disturbing to him. Often mutually exclusive are three kinds of satisfaction: getting the task done, having a happy time with others, or gaining some self-satisfying ends. This three-fold classification is drawn from theories of interpersonal behavior in organizations and forms the basis for the Ori.

The three scores obtained from the Ori reflect the three kinds of satisfaction.

The first is *self-orientation*. It reflects the extent a person describes himself as expecting direct rewards for himself regardless of the task the group is doing or the effects of what he does has upon others meeting with him. For him, a group is "literally a theatre in which certain generalized needs can be satisfied. The other members are both the remainder of the cast as well as an audience for which the self-orientation member can air his personal diffculties, gain esteem or status, aggress or dominate." A person with a high score in self-orientation is more likely to be rejected by others, to be introspective, to be dominating and to be unresponsive to the needs of others around him. He is concerned mainly with himself, not co-workers' needs or the job to be done.

The second score is *interaction-orientation*. It reflects the extent of a person's concern with maintaining happy, harmonious relationships in a group, often making it difficult for the person to contribute to the task at hand or to be of help to the other members. Interest in the group's activities is high but that interest is not ordinarily conducive to the progress of the group in completing its tasks.

Third is the *task-orientation* score. It reflects the extent to which a person is concerned about completing the group's task, working persistently, and doing the best job possible. In groups, despite his concern with the task, the task-oriented member tends to work hard within the group to make it as productive as possible. If he is interested in what the group is doing, he will fight hard for what he regards as right.

For self-orientation, Table 3 shows that there was no significant difference when the Koreans are compared to the other groups. All four groups had a similar concern for self in group interaction.

For interaction-orientation, the Koreans placed a lower emphasis on maintaning harmonious group relationships than did the Americans and Australians, being significantly different than both groups. When compared to the Japanese, there was no significant difference, suggesting both Koreans and Japanese viewed group harmony in a similar fashion.

Table 3   ORI COMPARISON ON SELF, INTERACTION AND TASK-ORIENTATIONS

Group	Mean	Standard Deviation	t value
1. Self-Orientation			
Koreans compared to:	23.93	4.98	
a. Americans	23.47	5.86	.49*
b. Australians	24.98	5.82	1.10*
c. Japanese	23.22	6.77	.67*
2. Interaction-Orientation			
Koreans Compared to:	26.07	4.61	
a. Amercans	28.70	6.66	2.52***
b. Australians	30.51	5.80	4.73**
c. Japanese	26.06	7.84	.01*
3. Task-Orientation			
Koreans compared to:	31.00	4.02	
a. Americans	28.83	6.44	2.17**
b. Australians	25.50	6.67	5.21**
c. Japanese	29.02	7.83	1.64*

N=Koreans-73; Americans-397; Australians-219; Japanese-504.
*N.S.D.   **p<.001   ***p<.05

For task-orientation, the Koreans differed significantly with the Americans and Australians but not the Japanese. The Koreans and Japanese apparently felt that the task was more important in group activties than did the Americans and the Australians, the latter two having placed greater stress on the social-emotional aspects.

What the Ori findings suggest is that Koreans are more prone to talk about task-related subjects and not to talk as much about matters that enhance group relations. This conclusion also seems to reflect the FIRO-B results which showed weaker inclusion and affection needs among the Koreans.

CONCLUSIONS

What do the results reveal about Korean oral communication patterns? The results support the observations of McQuerry; Cha, Choi, Suh; Oliver; and Klopf, Ishii and Cambra, mentioned earlier. In general, the Koreans tend to be talkative and to dominate oral encounters, certainly more so than the other groups studied. They hold a weaker inclusion need, comparatively speaking, than do the Americans and Australians, implying that this need is satisfied, quite likely as a result of stronger family bonds and friendships. But they apparently need to be in control of interpersonal transactions, more so than the Americans and Australians. And, as the Ori results indicate, they seem to place less emphasis on the social and emotional aspects of group interaction and more on the task at hand than the Americans and Australians. Yet, the Koreans are similar to the Japanese in several of the factors, specifically, the inclusion and control needs and the interaction-and task-orientations.

Although the results of the PVB, FIRO-B and Ori appear to confirm other studies about Korean speaking, they should be interpreted or utilized with reservation. This research was exploratory and further research, especially with Korean populations other than the one studied here, seems necessary.

Whatever future research is done, it should involve instruments and methodology applicable in all of the counries participating. The three instruments used in the research reported here were American contrived and tested for homogeneity, reliability and validity in North America. More suitable would be measures, currently not available, developed within each country and factor analyzed cross-culturally. From that analysis, the items which emerge as common to all cultures become the ones constituting the instrument. There are, of course, other methods of cross-cultural research that could be considered.

Regardless, the research reported here gives an understanding of the patterns of communication among Koreans and how the Korean patterns compare to those in America, Australia and Japan.

FOOTNOTES

1. B. McQuerry, "Koreans, a Rapidly Assimilated Group," *Asian-Americans in Hawaii* (Honolulu: General Assistance Center for the Pacific, University of Hawaii, 1975).
2. B.K. CHA, C.S. CHOI and C.W. SUH, "A Study of Americans' Attitudes Toward Koreans," *Korea Journal*, Vol. 16, No. 11, pp. 28-29.
3. R. Oliver, *Korea: Forgotten Nation* (Washington: Public Affairs Press, 1944).
4. D. KLOPF, S. ISHII and R. CAMBRA, "Speech Apprehension: A Comparison of Japanese, American, Australian and Korean College Students," *Otsuma Review*, in press.
5. C. DAVID MORTENSEN, PAUL H. ARNSTON and MYRONLUSTIG, "The Measurement of Verbal Predispositions: Scale Development and Application," *Human Communication Research*, 3, Winter 1977, pp. 146-158.
6. WILLIAM C. SCHUTZ, *The FIRO Scales-Manual* (Palo Alto, CA: Consulting Psychologists Press, Inc., 1976), pp. 3-19.
7. BERNARD M. BASS, *The Orientation Inventory-Manual*, research edition (Palo Alto, CA: Consulting Psychologists Press, Inc., 1962), pp. 3-20.
8. D. KLOPF, S. ISHII and R. CAMBRA, "Patterns of Oral Communication Among the Japanese, *Cross-Currents*, V, June 1978, pp. 37-49.
9. J. TUCCY, "T-Test Procedure," in N.H. Nie, C.H. Hall, J.G. Jenkins, K. Steinbrenner and D.H. Bent, eds., *Statistical Package for the Social Sciences* (New York: McGraw-Hill, 1975), pp. 267-275.
10. MORTENSEN, ARNSTON, LUSTIG, 146-158.
11. M.D. SCOTT and W.G. POWERS, *Interpersonal Communication: A Question of Needs* (Boston: Houghton Mifflin, 1978), pp. 3-15.
12. SCHUTZ, pp. 3-19.
13. BASS, pp. 3-20.

2. COMMUNICATION APPREHENSION IN SWITZERLAND, KOREA, AND THE UNITED STATES *

Myung-Seok Park
Dankook University

Annette M. Andrighetti
Gianni Mocellin
Donald W. Klopf
West Virginia University

---

* Paper prepared for the Fall 1992 World Communication Association Convention, Seoul, Korea

Research shows the extent of communication apprehension among people in many countries.[1] But in others, little is known.[2] This study attempts to broaden knowledge about communication apprehension in cultures not yet studied as it examines such apprehension in Switzerland and Korea, comparing them with Americans for study purposes.

Before reporting the findings, communication apprehension is explained and its negative impact on people's lives is noted, at least on the lives of the United States citizens since the research has been largely directed at that group and the conclusions have been well documented.[3]

ORAL APPREHENSION

Communication apprehension is a person's level of fear or anxiety associated with either real or anticipated talk with one or more persons. Those who have a high degree of apprehension experience fear or anxiety in almost every communication encounter or expected encounter. Not only do they suffer the common "stage fright" the average person feels when giving a speech to an audience, they are almost always fearful or anxious in all speaking situations including the public speaking situation. Their fear or anxiety surpasses any rewards they think they will get by talking, thus, they either do not speak at all or avoid speaking unless obligated to do so. When forced to speak, they appear to others as shy, non-assertive, nervous, embarrassed, uncomfortable and reticent. They respond negatively to any oral apprehension situation, real or anticipated, public or private, involving any number of people in small or large groups.[4] Because they tend to withdraw from or avoid communicating, they are not positively perceived at school, on the job or in social interactions.

ACADEMIC IMPLICATIONS

In the academic area, the research reveals characterizing behavior of the highly apprehensive. In school, highly apprehensive individuals tend to drop speech classes early in the semester, if they enroll at all.[5] They prefer large lecture classes over those small classes which encourage extensive student participation.[6] In the large classes, they choose seats in the back on the classroom's periphery. The seats front and center are most accessible to the teacher, and students in those seats are more likely to be called upon.[7] Should a class offer tutoring help or advising of any sort, high apprehensives are not likely to seek it.[8] Because they avoid talking, their fellow students ignore them, having learned to do so from trying to draw them into class discussions.[9] When the high apprehensives do participate, their comments often are irrelevant to the on-going discussion or their verbalizations differ from the others.[10] They are low producers of original ideas in group discussions.[11]

More devastating than their speech behavior is the feelings the others in the classroom have of them, others being both students and teachers. The other students perceive them as non-assertive, risk-avoiders, cooperative, non-directive, "go-along" persons, uncommunicative, hard-to-know and cool.[12] The highly apprehensive is seen as less socially attractive, less sexually attractive, less sociable, less competent, less task attractive and less composed than the other students.[13] They are rarely turned to for opinion leadership.[14]

Teachers expect the highly apprehensive to have lower overall academic achievement, less satisfactory relationships with others and a lower probability of success in future education than their less apprehensive peers.[15]

Within the academic environment, the results of the negativism toward high apprehensives have been established. The high apprehensives have lower overall college grade-point averages,[16] lower grades in small classes,[17] and lower achievement on standardized tests than the less apprehensive in spite of their intelligence level which in many cases is high.[18] Also, they develop a dislike for school early and dropout readily. Interestingly, high apprehensives are just as apprehensive when it comes to written communication.[19]

The support seems overwhelming; high apprehensives are negatively impacted in their academic life.

ECONOMIC IMPLICATIONS

In the employment area, the research reveals negative economic implications. Job applicants with excellent credentials but highly apprehensive were seen as less task and social attractive than those with low apprehension. They were projected as going to be less satisfied in their job, to have poorer relationships with their work peers, supervisors and subordinates, to be less productive, and have less likelihood for advancement. In addition, high apprehensives are less likely to be offered an interview and, even if they are interviewed, they would be less likely to be hired than low apprehensives.[20]

High apprehensives prefer positions with lower pay and status than jobs with higher pay and status but involving higher communication requirements,[21] as state and federal government employees actually demonstrated.[22] Of course, high apprehensives work. However, they do not often find a job which is pleasing to them,[23] or do they stay on the job as long as low apprehensives.[24]

While much more study needs to be done on the economic implications, the evidence accumulated so far seems to clearly support the proposition that high apprehensives are negatively affected on the job.

SOCIAL IMPLICATIONS

The effect of high apprehension on a person's social life follows the patterns already described. High apprehensives interact less with peers, strangers, engage in more exclusive dating,[25] marry more quickly after graduation from college,[26] prefer housing remote from others,[27] and register and vote less than their low apprehensive peers.[29]

Communication apprehension has been found to be correlated

with a variety of socially undesirable personality characteristics. A series of studies show that self-esteem and communication apprehension were negatively correlated for samples of college students, for elementary and secondary school teachers and for a group of federal employees. High communication apprehension was associated with negative self-image in every sample. Also, communication apprehension was found to be positively correlated with general anxiety and negatively correlated with cyclothymia, emotional maturity, dominance, surgency, character, adventurousness, confidence, self-control and trustfulness.[30] Unfortunately, the overall relationship shows communication apprehension to be associated with the socially maladaptive end of the continuum on all the personality variables with which a significant relationship was observed. There is one encouraging observation: no significant relationship exists between apprehension and intelligence. Thus, although high communication apprehensives have a negative image of themselves, they are not intellectually different from persons with lower communication apprehension.[31] Again, the evidence supports the proposition that the effects of high communication apprehension results in a negative impact on a person's academic, economic and social life.

APPREHENSION LEARNED

What causes communication apprehension? While all of the causes are not fully known, it is clear that communication apprehension is not hereditary. Highly apprehensive parents do not necessarily produce highly apprehensive children. On the contrary, the evidence suggests that communication apprehension is learned by the individual, usually during the early childhood years. When the child is positively reinforced for speaking, it appears unlikely that the child will become highly apprehensive. With positive reinforcement, the child learns to value speech both as a tool and as an intrinsically desirable experience.

The child who is not reinforced for speaking, or is punished, fails to develop the normal apprehension for oral commun-cation. The child does not find reward in communication itself, nor learns the instrumental functions of communication. For such a child, commu-nication is not a tool. Rather, communicating results in negative experiences. Such a child is likely to develop a high level of commu-nication apprehension.

While the nature of reinforcement during early childhood is the principle causative factor which leads to or prevents the development of communication apprehension, it is not the only possible cause. A traumatic experience can alter the normal speech pattern of a child and lead to the development of high apprehension. The loss of a par-ent, brother or sister, particularly through violence, can severely dis-turb a child. A result of such a disturbance could be the development of high communication apprehension.

Usually high communication apprehension develops in preschool years or does not develop at all. However, there are instances where it develops later, or develops early but is eliminated during early school years. Each of these effects can be attributed to the impact of the school environment—teachers and peers. For the child who has experienced negative reinforcement in the pre-shcool years and enters school as a high communication apprehensive, extensive posi-tive reinforcement from teachers and later from peers can help over-come the problem. However, such positive reinforcement is not always provided. Similarly, a child may enter school as a moderate communication apprehensive but negative reinforcement from teachers and peers may cause the level of communication apprehension to increase. Neither of these effects will occur quickly, and the change in the child may be hardly noticeable, even to a trained observer. Patterns which have developed over several years prior to entering school are seldom reversed in a single year.[32]

Fensterheim and Baer sum up the causes in these remarks:

> Parents, teachers, clergymen and businessmen have unwittingly conspired to produce a nation of timid souls. In early years, many mothers and fathers cen-

sor the child who decides to speak up for his rights and thus, hinder the child's assertion of self. Teachers reward the student who does not question the educational system and deal sternly with those who buck it. In most cases the church fosters the idea of humility and sacrifice rather than standing up for self. Many an employee learns early in his career that if he "speaks up," he is not likely to receive a raise or promotion and may even lose his job. Adopted at the office, this attitude carries over to home and social life.[33]

Children are trained to be silent and much of society reinforces that training.

COMPARISONS OF SWISS/KOREANS/AMERICANS

This study's purpose is to determine the incidence of communication apprehension among Swiss and Korean university students and to compare the findings with that of an American student population. To do so, the Personal Report of Communication Apprehension (PRCA-24) was administered to Swiss, Korean and American students.

The PRCA-24 consists of 24 self-report items scored on a Likert-type scale (Appendix A). Individual scores can range from 24 to 120, with scores above 24 indicating a degree of apprehension. The PRCA-24 is in English and the student sample was able to comprehend the language so the scale required no translation. The sample was made up of students from the University of Geneva, Hankuk University of Foreign Studies in Seoul and various universities in the United States. Scale reliabilities were found to be .93 for Switzerland, .95 for Korea, and .96 for the United States.

The results of t test comparisons of the three cultures indicate that the Koreans (M=52.78, SD=10.59) are significantly less apprehensive than the Swiss (M=65.85, SD=17.86) and the Americans (M=65.60, SD=15.30; p<.001). No significant difference appeared between the Swiss and the Americans.

The PRCA-24 allows for an analysis of apprehension in four speaking situations—dyadic (two-person talk), meetings, small group, and public speaking situations. Comparisons using the t test in the four situations show the Koreans as less apprehensive than the Swiss and the Americans but the Swiss and Americans as not significantly different.

DISCUSSION

The study compared the incidence of communication apprehension as perceived among persons from Korea, Switzerland and the United States. The results conclude the Koreans perceive themselves less apprehensive than the Swiss and the Americans when interacting with others in communication situations. This conclusion should be considered tentative. The Korean sample consists of students from one Korean institution, Hankuk University of Foreign Studies, who perhaps are above average, being part of an elite group of foreign language specialists. However, the literature does suggest that Koreans are orally assertive people, often portrayed as out-going and talkative. They are judged to be relatively active, aggressive, pleasant, industrious, friendly, and fast,[34] being perceived as aggressive, conspicuous and more tempermental than other Orientals.[35]

Perhaps several hundred years of a strong village government system partially accounts for the oral expressiveness. The system stressed democratic self-government which fostered the individual expression of opinion. Parliamentary procedure proved vital in the discussion of community problems and it was taught in church organizations to permit free yet orderly discussions.[36] "Critical and selective patriotism," according to an analyst, is on the increase in Korea as contrasted to a blind loyalty to the nation-state.[37] And, independence, not only of the country, but for the individual as well, has been emphasized throughout Korea's history.[38]

The Korean findings at best are speculative. Research on the oral communication behavior of Koreans has not been extensive and our efforts appear to be pioneer in nature. While this study's results portray orally assertive people, much more research is necessary before more positive conclusions can be drawn.

The Swiss and American results indicate that the two groups are similar in terms of their perceived degree of communication apprehension. Both cultures are heterogeneous, mixing persons of varied European backgrounds, although the United States is becoming heavily populated by persons from Oriental stock. Orientals participating in the study were limited in number and very likely natives of the United States.

The Swiss and Americans, when compared to other cultures previously studied, perceive themselves to be not significantly different than Australians, Micronesians, Chinese and Filipinos, but significantly more apprehensive than Taiwanese and significantly less apprehensive than Japanese.[39] The results are speculative; however, the sample sizes are small and populations of university students probably are not characteristic of the general population in any of the countries.

PERSONAL REPORT OF COMMUNICATION APPREHENSION *

This instrument is composed of twenty-four statements concerning feelings about communicating with other people. Please indicate the degree to which each statement applies to you by marking whether you (1) strongly agree, (2) agree, (3) are undecided, (4) disagree, (5) strongly disagree. Please just record your first impression.

1. I dislike participating in group discussions.
2. Generally, I am comfortable while participating in group discussions.
3. I am tense and nervous while participating in group discus-sions.
4. I like to get involved in group discussions.
5. Engaging in a group discussion with new people makes me tense and nervous.
6. I am calm and relaxed while participating in group discussions.
7. Generally, I am nervous when I have to participate in a meeting.
8. Usually I am calm and relaxed while participating in meetings.
9. I am very calm and relaxed when I am called upon to express an opinion at a meeting.
10. I am afraid to express myself at meetings.
11. Communicating at meetings usually makes me uncomfortable.
12. I am very relaxed when answering questions at a meeting.
13. While participating in a conversation with a new aquaintance, I feel very nervous.
14. I have no fear of speaking up in conversations.
15. Ordinarily, I am very tense and nervous in conversations.
16. Ordinarily, I am very calm and relaxed in conversations.
17. While conversing with a new aquaintance, I feel very relaxed.
18. I' m afraid to speak up in conversations.

---

* J.C. McCroskey, V.P. Richmond, *Communication: Apprehension, Avoidance, and Effectiveness*, II, 123-125.

19. I have no fear of giving a speech.
20. Certain parts of my body feel tense and rigid while giving a speech.
21. I feel relaxed while giving a speech.
22. My thoughts become confused and jumbled when I am giving a speech.
23. I face the prospect of giving a speech with confidence.
24. While giving a speech, I get so nervous I forget facts I really know.

FOOTNOTES

1. J.C. McCroskey, "Oral Communication Apprehension: A Summary of Recent Theory and Research," *Human Communication Research*, IV (Fall 1977), 79-80.
2. In D. Klopf and S. Ishii, "A Comparison of the Communication Activities of Japanese and American Adults," *ELEC Bulletin*, 53 (Spring 1976), and S. Ishii, R. Cambra and D. Klopf, "Communication Anxiety: A Comparison of Japanese and American College Students," *Otsuma Review*, 10 (January 1978), 86-94.
3. McCroskey, 85.
4. McCroskey, 78-80.
5. J.C. McCroskey, "Measures of Communication Bound Anxiety," *Speech Monographs*, XXXVII (November 1970), 269-277.
6. J.C. McCroskey and J.F. Andersen, "The Relationship Between Communication Apprehension and Academic Achievement Among College Students," *Human Communication Research*, III (Fall 1976), 73-81.
7. J.C. McCroskey and R.W. McVetta, "Classroom Seating Arrangements: Instructional Communication Theory Versus Student Preferences," *Communication Education*, XXVII (March 1978), 99-111.
8. M.D. Scott, M. Yates and L.R. Wheeless, "An Exploratory Investigation of the Effects of Communcation Apprehension in Alternative Systems of Instruction," International Communication Association convention paper, Chicago, 1975.
9. McCroskey, "Oral Communication Apprehension: A Summary of Recent Theory and Research," 86.
10. A.N. Weiner, *Machiavellianism as a Predictor of Group Interaction*, M.A. Thesis, West Virginia University.
11. F.M. Jablin and L. Sussman, "Correlates of Individual Productivity in Real Brainstorming Groups," Speech Communication Association convention paper,San Francisco, 1976.
12. D. Merrill, *Reference Survey Profile* (Denver: Personal Predictions and Research, Inc., 1974).
13. J.C. McCroskey, J.A. Daly, V.P. Richmond and R.L. Falcione, "Studies of the Relationship Between Communication Apprehension and Self Esteem," *Human Communication Research*, III (Spring 1977), 269-277.
14. H.R. Witteman, *The Relationship of Communication Apprehension to Opinion Leadership and Innovativeness*, M.A. Thesis, West Virginia University.
15. J.C. McCroskey and J. Daly, "Teachers' Expectations of the Communication Apprehensive Child in the Elementary School," *Human Communication Research* III (Fall 1976), 67-72.
16. McCroskey and Andersen, "The Relationship Between Communication Apprehension and Academic Achievement Among College Students," 78.
17. H.T. Hurt, R. Preiss and B. Davis, "The Effect of Communication Apprehension of Middle-School Children on Sociometric Choice, Affective and Cognitive Learning," International Communication Association convention paper, Portland, 1976.
18. McCroskey and Andersen, "The Relationship Between Communication

Apprehension an Academic Achievement Among College Students," 78.
19. McCroskey, "Oral Communication Apprehension: A Summary of Recent Theory and Research," 90.
20. V.P. Richmond, "Communication Apprehension and Success in the Job Applicant Screening Process," International Communication Association convention paper, Berlin, 1977, and J.A. Daly and S. Leth, "Communication Apprehension and the Personal Selection Decision," International Communication Association convention paper, Portland, 1976.
21. J.A. Daly and J.C. McCroskey, "Occupational Choice and Desirability as a Function of Communication Apprehension," *Journal of Counseling Psychology*, XXII (August 1975), 309-313.
22. M.D. Scott, J.C. McCroskey and M.E. Sheahan, "Measuring Communication Apprehension," *Journal of Communication*, XXVIII (Winter 1978), 106.
23. R.L. Falcione, J.C. McCroskey and J. Daly, "Job Satisfaction as a Function of Employee's Communcation Apprehension, Self-Esteem, and Perceptions of Their Immediate Supervisors," *Communication Yearbook I*, Brent D. Ruben, Ed. (Brunswick, NJ: Transaction Books, 1977), 363-375.
24. Scott, McCroskey and Sheahan, 106.
25. J.C. McCroskey and M.E. Sheahan, "Communication Apprehension, Social Preference and Social Behavior in a College Environment," *Communication Quarterly*, in press.
26. J.C. McCroskey and M.M. Kretzschmar, "Communication Apprehension and Marital Relationships of College Graduates," Eastern Communication Association convention paper, New York, 1977.
27. J.C. McCroskey and T. Leppard, "The Effects of Communication Apprehension on Nonverbal Behavior," Eastern Communication Association convention paper, New York, 1975.
28. M.E. Sheahan, *Communication Apprehension and Electoral Participation*, M.A. Thesis, West Virginia University.
29. J.C. McCroskey and V.P. Richmond, "Self-Credibility as an Index of Self-Esteem," Speech Communication Association convention paper, Houston, 1975.
30. J.C. McCroskey, J.A. Daly and G.A. Sorensen, "Personality Correlates of Communication Apprehension," *Human Communication Research*, II (Summer 1976), 376-380.
31. McCroskey, Daly and Sorensen, 376-380. While the research presented here supports the position that communication apprehension offers disagreeable consequences, we should recognize that this viewpoint may not be shared by the apprehensive. Most apprehensives, especially adults, quite likely have adjusted to their lives and have made choices in job, housing, and mate that are compatible with their apprehension level. As a consequence, they may be quite happy. On the other hand, we should recognize that low apprehensives may not live ideal lives. They may be so success oriented that they have become unhappy in the process.
32. J.C. McCroskey, "The Problem of Communication Apprehension in the Classroom," *Communication*, IV (June 1976), Convention Edition, 117-119.
33. H. Fensterheim and J. Baer, *Don't Say Yes When You Want to Say No*. (New

York: Dell Pub., Co., 1975), 20-21.

34. Bae-Keun Cha, Chang-Sup Choi and Chung-Woo Suh, "A Study of Americans' Attitudes Toward Korea," *Korea Journal*, 16 (November, 1976), 28-29.

35. Bernice Kim McQuerry, "Koreans, A Rapidly Assimilated Group," *Asian-Americans in Hawaii*, Nancy Foon Young, ed., General Assistance Center for the Pacific, University of Hawaii, Honolulu, 1975.

36. Robert T. Oliver, *Korea: Forgotten Nation* (Washington: Public Affairs Press, 1944), 106.

37. Young-Ho Lee, "The Korean People's National Consciousness: An Analysis of Survey Data," *Korea Journal*, 18 (January 1978), 47.

38. Oliver, 18-19.

39. Donald W. Klopf and Ronald E. Cambra, "Communication Apprehension in the Pacific Basin", A paper presented at the North South Intercultural Communication Conference, Chula, Mexico, December 19-21, 1983.

3. CULTURAL DIFFERENCES IN TACTILE AVOIDANCE: KOREAN AND AMERICAN UNIVERSITY STUDENTS COMPARED*

Myung-Seok Park
Dankook University

Donald W.Klopf
West Virginia University

Beth A.Casteel
West Virginia University

---

* Paper prepared for the June 1992 World Communication Association — Korea Convention, Seoul, Korea

Touch is the first form of communicative interaction experienced by humans. Prior to and at birth, an infant is being touched—by the mother in her body and by the person performing the delivery. In the early days of life, touch continues to play a vital communicative role (Frank, 1957; Montagu, 1971). This prominence of infantile contact could be the reason the drive for physical contact is strong in people's lives, being as intense as the need for food (Harlow, 1958). Denied contact, a child's emotional, intellectual, social, and physical development may be abnormal (Spitz, 1945). For the blind and the deaf, touch is a principal means of communication. Even persons without such handicaps rely on touch to communicate. It can communicate warmth and love. Moreover it can transmit dislike as fist fighters can attest (Jourard, 1966; Rosenfeld, Kartus, & Ray, 1976).

With touch an important factor in human communication, considerable research has centered on it. Much of the research, however, has revolved around touch as a sensory modality. But in recent years, interest in the role of touch in communication has grown in one specific area, the area of attention here, that of touch avoidance (Andersen & Leibowitz, 1978). The interest has been confined to the United States of America up to this juncture. The research reported here extends the interest in touch avoidance cross-culturally, comparing Korea and the United States on the matter.

TACTILE COMMUNICATIVE BEHAVIOR

Tactile communicative behavior is defined generally to mean the laying on of some body part so as to feel one's self, other persons, or objects of any sort. The person touching perceives through the sense of feel, a feeling which can be both physical and emotional (Montagu, 1971). A caress from a loved one, for example, can evoke the physical sensation of touching the other person and it also can evoke an emotional experience of loving attention.

Tactile communicative behavior sends various messages. These range from an impersonal sort of touch to the very personal. At the impersonal level is a *functional/professional* touch in which touch is incidental to the purpose of the communicative interaction. The receivers of touching at this level accept it because they understand it is necessary in completing a service. A doctor or dentist, for example, must touch a patient as a function of the profession, as part of the diagnosis or operation being conducted. A hairdresser or shoe salesperson touches in the same professional sense.

A less impersonal form of touch is the *social/polite* level. It is used to neutralize status differences between several people or to affirm the existence of another individual. Two business people may shake hands to acknowledge respect for one another. A teacher might touch a student while discussing an important issue.

A more personal sort of touch is the *friendship/warmth* tactile behavior. It is used to show others that they are valued and respected. Individuals often demonstrate affection for their friends through a pat on the back, a hug, or an embrace. An even more personal touch is the *love/intimacy* touch signaling closeness with persons intensely affectionate. Touch at this level may include caressing, kissing, hugging, and often sexual activity although such activity is not what makes people intimate. Opposite sex friends who have an intense affectionate concern for each other will practice love/intimacy touching.

The most personal type is *sexual arousal*. This type may take place in the bounds of an intimate relationship but may also occur in the presence of two strangers, for instance, in an act of prostitution or a night of pleasure between two strangers. Sexual arousal is the most intense form of tactile communication and normally provides more personal satisfaction than the other types (Heslin, 1982).

Touch usage varies across cultures. Some cultures allow much touching to occur and these have been termed *contact cultures*. Those in which touching is limited are called *non-contact cultures* (Hall, 1959, 1966). Persons from contact cultures interact at closer proximity to each other. They touch more, face one another more directly, and utilize more eye contact than those in the non-contact cultures. Contact cultures tend to include most Arab countries,

Mediterranean and Jewish people, Eastern Europeans, Russians, Hispanics, and Indonesians. The non-contact peoples are typical of Northern Europe, the United States, Japan, China, Korea, and other countries in the Far East (Andersen, 1990; Remland & Jones, 1988; Argyle, 1972). Each culture has its own norms for proper tactile behavior (Frank, 1957).

TOUCH AVOIDANCE

Research in the United States has uncovered a group of people known as *touch avoidant*—persons who feel uncomfortable in situations requiring touch of some sort. They have negative feelings toward touching (Andersen & Leibowitz, 1978; Andersen, Andersen, & Lustig, 1987; Andersen & Sull, 1985). Touch avoidance is not a reference to how much a person actually touches, but an index of a person's affect toward touching (Deethardt & Hines, 1983).

Touch avoidance is not necessarily a characteristic of contact or non-contact cultures, although the presumption is that non-contact cultures will have more touch avoidant people. The known research has not explored cross-cultural touch avoidance. But touch avoidance has been the subject of considerable gender research, albeit much is inconclusive.

Major reviews of touch avoidant research by Major (1981) and Stier and Hall (1984) point up the contradictory nature of research findings regarding variations between men and women in tactile behavior. Only two findings are supported by the research. One states that touch between women is more common than between men. The other concludes that women are more likely to be touched than men (Major Schmidlin & Williams, 1990).

Henley (1973, 1973, 1977) in examining dominance and submission patterns in nonverbal behavior suggests a reason for the gender touching patterns. Henley argues that a superior status person is more likely to touch lower status person than the opposite, and the touching behavior of the superior status person is more acceptable whereas the opposite probably is not. Henley contends, therefore, that men initiate touch with women more often than women initiate touch with men because of the superior status of men in Western society. Major (1981) and Maier and Ernest (1978) support Henley's argument, noting that from infancy women are touched more than men, that men initiate more touch to women, and that women react more positively than men to touch initiated by an equal status other.

KOREAN/AMERICAN RESEARCH

The lack of conclusive data regarding touch avoidant behavior caused Andersen and Leibowitz (1978) to construct the Touch Avoidance Instrument. This instrument measures the degree to which persons perceive themselves touching persons of the same sex and of the opposite sex. It was employed in this study to measure same and opposite sex touch avoidant behavior between persons in Korea and the United States.

University students from the two cultures participated in the research reported here. The Korean respondents (240 men and women) represented Dankook University in Seoul and the Americans (273 men and women) came from West Virginia University in Eastern United States. They were similar in years in school and age. Both groups completed the Touch Avoidance Instrument on their respective campuses during the 1992-1993 academic year.

Touch avoidance scores were obtained from each respondent in same-sex interactions and opposite-sex interactions. The higher the scores in each type of interaction, the more touch avoidant were the respondents.

RESEARCH RESULTS

Statistical analyses of the data obtained from the Korean and American respondents revealed significant differences in same-sex interactions, Koreans (M=29.64, SD=5.50) and Americans(M=32.38,

SD= 6.53), *t*= 4.83, *p*<.001, and in opposite-sex interactions, Koreans (*M*=19.00, *SD*= 6.55) and Americans(*M*= 15.02, *SD*=4.62), *t*=7.72, *p*<.001. Across cultures, within gender, significant differences also appeared: same-sex persons, Korean women (*M*=26.83, *SD*=5.35) and American women (*M*= 29.56, *SD*=6.60), *t*=2.38, *p*<.05; Korean men (*M*=30.34, *SD*= 5.32) and American men (*M*=34.30, *SD*=5.75), *t*=6.37, *p*<.0 01; opposite-sex persons, Korean women (*M*=26.88, *SD*=5.54), American women (*M*= 16.09, *SD*=4.27), *t*=12.07, *p*<.06 Korean men (*M*=17.03, *SD*=5.16) and American men(*M*=14.27, *SD*=4.72), *t*=4.98, *p*<.001. Within cultures, significant differences appeared between the men and women: same-sex persons, Korean men (*M*=30.34, *SD*=5.32) and Korean women (*M*= 26.83, *SD*=5.35), *t*=3.82, *p*<.005, and American men (*M*= 34.30, *SD*=5.75) and American women(*M*=29.56, *SD*=6.60), *t*=6.07, *p*<.001; opposite-sex persons, Korean women (*M*=26.88, *SD*=5.54) and Korean men (*M*=17.03, *SD*=5.16), *t*=10.98, *p*< .001, and American women (*M*=16.09, *SD*=4.27,) and American men(*M*=14.27, *SD*=4.72), *t*= 3.17, *p*<.05

The results are conclusive. Cross-culturally, in terms of touch avoidance in same-sex interactions Americans are more reluctant to touch than are Koreans, American women are more reluctant to touch than are Korean women, and American men are more reluctant to touch than are Korean men. Cross-culturally, in terms of opposite-sex interactions, Koreans are more reluctant to touch than are Americans, Korean women are more reluctant to touch than are American women, and Korean men are more reluctant to touch than are American men. Within cultures in terms of same-sex interactions, Korean men are more reluctant to touch Korean men than Korean women are in touching Korean women, and American men are more reluctant to touch American men than American women are in touching American women. Within cultures, in terms of opposite-sex interactions, Korean women are more reluctant to touch Korean men than Korean men are in touching Korean women, and American women are more reluctant to touch American men than American men are in touching American women.

DISCUSSION

Significant differences are obvious between the Korean and American perceptions of their touch avoidant behavior, the Koreans being less touch avoidant than the Americans. Thus, Koreans touch more when they are conversing with other people, be they of the same sex or opposite sex, than do Americans. Whether this conclusion means the Koreans are to be included among the contact cultures is unknown. No basis for judgment exists. No known touch avoidant research has been completed in other cultures to date, hence, comparisons are not possible that could give greater insight. However, the literature that does exist, based on field research studies, places both Koreans and Americans among the non-contact cultures as previously indicated.

Significant differences also are obvious in terms of gender. The research indicates that men are more willing to touch women than women are willing to touch men. But men are not as eager to touch other men as women are to touch other women. These conclusions are supported by the research reported earlier in this study. Whether these conclusions support the contention offered previously that men initiate touch with women more often than women initiate touch with men because of the superior status of men is unknown. The research mentioned earlier in this paper would suggest that women perceive men as superior. This research can neither confirm or deny that argument.

Limitations preclude generalizing the results obtained here to the general populations in Korea and the United States. The results are limited to small samples of college students in both cultures and these samples may or may not be reflective of the entire population in either culture. Further research would be necessary to determine whether these samples are reflective of the total population.

Then, too, the instrument used in the research calls for the perceptions of the respondents to the sampling items. A far better measure would be field observations of actual communicative interactions. Such observation is virtually impossible, hence, the use of the Touch Avoidance Instrument.

These and other limitations make the results questionable. However, in terms of the gender findings, enough other research evidence exists to suggest that those findings are confirmed. Men do not like to touch men as much as women like to touch women and women are touched by men more than women touch men.

TOUCH AVOIDANCE INSTRUMENT 10

Sex: Male _____ Age: _____ Class standing: _____
     Female _____

DIRECTIONS: This instrument is composed of 18 statements concerning feelings about touching other people and being touched. Please indicate the degree to which each statement applies to you by circling whether you (1) Strongly agree, (2) Agree, (3) Are undecided, (4) Disagree, or (5) Strongly disagree with each statement. While some of these statements may seem repetitious, take your time and try to be as honest as possible.

1. A hug from a same-sex friend is a true sign of friendship.   1 2 3 4 5

2. Opposite sex friends enjoy it when I touch them.   1 2 3 4 5

3. I often put my arm around friends of the same sex.   1 2 3 4 5

4. When I see two people of the same sex hugging, it revolts me.   1 2 3 4 5

5. I like it when members of the opposite sex touch me.   1 2 3 4 5

6. People shouldn't be so uptight about touching persons of the same sex.   1 2 3 4 5

7. I think it is vulgar when members of the opposite sex touch me.   1 2 3 4 5

8. When a member of the opposite sex touches me, I find it unpleasant.   1 2 3 4 5

9. I wish I were free to show emotions by touching members of the same sex.   1 2 3 4 5

10. I'd enjoy giving a massage to an opposite sex friend.   1 2 3 4 5

11. I enjoy kissing persons of the same sex.   1 2 3 4 5

12. I like to touch friends that are the same sex as I am.   1 2 3 4 5

13. Touching a friend of the same sex does not make me uncomfortable.   1 2 3 4 5

14. I find it enjoyable when my date and I embrace.   1 2 3 4 5

15. I enjoy getting a back rub from a member of the opposite sex.   1 2 3 4 5

16. I dislike kissing relatives of the same sex.   1 2 3 4 5

17. Intimate touching with members of the opposite sex is pleasurable.   1 2 3 4 5

18. I find it difficult to be touched by a member of my own sex.   1 2 3 4 5

BIBLIOGRAPHY OF REFERENCE MATERIALS ON TOUCH

Andersen, J.F., Andersen, P.A. & Lustig, M.W. (1987). Opposite Sex Touch Avoidance: a National Replication and Extension. *Journal of Nonverbal Behavior, 11(2)*, 89-109.

Andersen, P.A. (1990). Explaining Intercultural Differences in Nonverbal Communication. In L.A. Samovar and R.E. Porter (Eds.), *Intercultural Communication: a Reader*, sixth edition, (pp. 286-296). Belmont, CA: Wadsworth, Inc.

Andersen, P.A. & Knarr, L. (1989). Avoiding Communication: Verbal and Nonverbal Dimensions of Defensiveness. (Report No. CS-506-565) Paper presented at the Annual Meeting of the Western Speech Communication Association, Spokane, WA. (ERIC Document Reproduction Service No. ED (304-727).

Andersen, P.A. & Leibowitz, K. (1978). The Development and Nature of the Construct Touch Avoidance. *Environmental Psychology and Nonverbal Behavior, 3*, 89-106.

Andersen, P.A. & Sull, K.K. (1985). Out of Touch, out of Reach: Tactile Predispositions as Predictors of Interpersonal Distance. *Western Journal of Speech Communication, 49*, 57-72.

Argyle, M. (1972). Nonverbal Commnunication in Human Social Interaction. In R.A. Hinde (Ed.), *Non-verbal Communication*, (pp. 243-270). London, England: University Press.

Argyle, M. (1975). *Bodily Communication*. New York, NY: International Universities Press, 1975.

Barnlund, D.C. (1975). *Public and Private Self in Japan and the United States*. Tokyo, Japan: The Simul Press, Inc.

Burgoon, J.K. (1985,. Nonverbal Signals. In M.L. Knapp & G.R. Miller (Eds.), *Handbook of Interpersonal Communication*, (pp. 344-392). Beverly Hills: Sage Publications, Inc.

Clark, G. (1983). *Understanding the Japanese*. Tokyo, Japan.: Kinseido.

Crane, P.S. (1967). *Korean Patterns*. Seoul, Korea: Hollym Corporation Publishers.

Deethardt, J.F. & Hines, D.G. (1983). Tactile Communication and Personality Differences. *Journal of Nonverbal Behavior, 8(2)*, 143-156.

Derlega, V.J., Lewis, R.J., Harrison, S., Winstead, B.A. & Costanza, R. (1989). Gender Differences in the Initiation and Attribution of Tactile Intimacy. *Journal of Nonverbal Behavior, 13*, 83-97.

Doi, L.T. (1973). The Japanese Patterns of Communication and the Concept of Amae. *The Quarterly Journal of Speech, 59*, 180-185.

Fisher, J.D., Rytting, M. & Heslin, R. (1976). Hands Touching Hands: Affective and Evaluative Effects of an Interpersonal Touch. *Sociometry, 39*, 416-421.

Frank, L.K. (1957). Tactile Communication. *Genetic Psychology Monographs, 56*, 209-256.

Hall, E.T. (1959). *The Silent Language*. Garden City, NY: Anchor Press/Doubleday.

Hall, E.T. (1966). *The Hidden Dimension*. Garden City, Doubleday, Inc.

Hall, J.A. (1984). *Nonverbal Sex Differences*. Baltimore, MD: The Johns Hopkins University Press.

Hall, J.A. and Veccia, E.M. (1990). More "Touching" Observations: New Insights on Men, Women and Interpersonal Touch. *Journal of Personality and Social Psychology, 59,* 1155-1162.

Harlow, H.F. (1958). The Nature of Love. *American Psychologist. 13,* 673-685.

Harper, R.G. Wiens, A.N. Matarazzo, J.D. (1978). *Nonverval Communication: the State of the Art.* New York, NY: John Wiley & Sons.

Henley, N.M. (1973) . The Politics of Touch. In M. Brown (Ed.) *Radical Psychology,* (pp. 421-433). New York, NY: Harper Colophon Books.

Henley, N.M. (1973). Status and Sex: Some Touching Observations. *Bulletin of the Psychonomic Society, 2,* 91-93.

Henley, N.M. (1977). *Body Politics.* Englewood Cliffs, NJ: Prentice-Hall, Inc.

Heslin, R. & Patterson, M.L. (1982). *Nonverbal Behavior and Social Psychology.* New York, NY: Plenum Press.

Heslin, R. & Patterson, M.L. (1982). *Nonverbal Behavior and Social Psychology.* New York, NY: Plenum Press.

Jones, S. (1986). Sex Differences in Touch Communication. *The Western Journal of Speech Communication, 50,* 227-241.

Jourard, S.M. (1966). An Exploratory Study of Body-Accessibility *British Journal of Social Clinical Psychology,* 5, 221-231.

Jourard, S.M. & Rubin, J.E. (1968). Self-disclosure and Touching: a Study of Two Modes of Interpersonal Encounter and Their Interrelation. *Journal of Humanistic Psychology, 8,* 39-48.

Kim, H. &. Park, H.K. (Eds.). (1980). *Studies on Korea: a Scholar's Guide.* Honolulu, HI: University of Hawaii Press.

Klopf, D. & Ishii, S. (1937). *Communicating without Words.* Tokyo Japan: Nan 'un' do.

Klopf, D. (1991). Japanese Communication Practices: Recent Comparative Research. *Communication Quarterly, 39,* 130-143. Korean Overseas Information Service, Ministry of Culture and Information. (1979). *A Handbook of Korea.* Seoul, Korea: Seoul International Publishing House.

Korean Overseas Information Service. (1987). *A Handbook of Korea.* Seoul, Korea: Seoul International Publishing House.

Lebra, T.S. (1976). *Japanese Patterns of Behavior.* Honolulu, HI: The University Press.

Lebra, T.S. & Lebra, W.P. (Eds.) (1986) *Japanese Culture and Behavior.* Honolulu, HI: University of Hawai Press.

Leibowitz, K. & Andersen, P.A. (1980). The Development and Nature of the Construct Touch Avoidance. In B.W. Morse and L.A. Phelps (Eds.), *Interpersonal Communication: a Relational Perspective,* (pp. 213-229). Minneapolis, MN: Brooks Cole.

Lopez, A. (1973). *The Puerto Rican Papers.* Indianapolis IN: The Bobbs-Merrill Company, Inc.

Maier, R.A. & Ernest, R.C. (1978). Sex Differences in the Perception of Touching. *Perceptual and Motor Skills,* 46, 577-578.

Major, B. (1981). Gender Patterns in Touching Behavior. In C. Mayo and N.M. Henley (Eds.), *Gender and Nonverbal Behavior*, (pp. 15-34). New York, NY: Springer-Verlag.

Major, B., Schmidlin, A.M. & Williams, L. (1990). Gender Patterns in Social Touch: the Impact of Setting and Age. *Journal of Personality and Social Psychology, 58*, 634-643.

McCroskey, J.C., Fayer, J.M. & Richmond, V.P. (1985). Don' t speak to me in English: Communication Apprehension in Puerto Rico. *Communication Quarterly, 33*, 185-192.

Mehrabian, A. (1972). *Nonverbal Communication*. Chicago, IL: Aldine-Atherton, Inc.

Mehrabian, A. (1981). *Silent Messages*. Belmont, CA: Wadsworth Publishing Co. (first edition published in 1971).

Mills, C.W., Senior, C. & Goldsen, R.K.. (1967). *The Puerto Rican Journey*. New York, NY: Russell & Russell. (Original work published in 1950).

Montagu, A. (1971). *Touching: the Human Significance of the Skin*. New York, NY: Columbia University Press.

Morris, D. (1971). *Intimate Behavior*. New York, NY: Random House.

Morris, D. (1377). *Manwatching* New York, NY: Harry N. Abrams Inc.

Neustupny, J.V. (1987). *Communicating with the Japanese*. Tokyo Japan: The Japan Times.

Nguyen, T., Hesin, R. & Nguyen, M.L. (1975). The Meanings of Touch: Sex Differences. *Journal of Communication, 25*, 92-103.

Nine-Curt, C.J. (1984). *Non-verbal Communication in Puerto Rico*. (Report No. FL-015-096). Evaluation, Dissemination and Assessment Center for Bilingual Education, Cambridge, MA. (ERIC Document ED 258-468).

Okabe, R. (1983). Cultural Assumptions of East and West: Japan and the United States. In W.B. Gudykunst (Ed.). *Intercultural Communication Theory*, (pp. 21-44). Beverly Hills, CA: Sage Publications.

O' Mara, J. (1990). Reach out and Touch Someone: Tactile Communication in Selected Puerto Rican Novels. (Report No. CS 507-220). Paper presented at the annual meeting of the Eastern Communication Association, Philadelphia, PA. (ERIC Document Reproduction Service No. ED 321-324).

Park, M-S. (1979). *Communication Syles in Two Cultures: Korean. and American*. Seoul, Korea: Han Shin Publishing Co.

Patterson, M.L. (1978). The Role of Space in Social Interaction. In A.W. Siegman and S. Feldstein (Eds.), *Nonverbal Behavior and Communication*, (pp. 265-290). Hillsdale, NJ: Lawrence Erlbaum Associates, Publishers.

Pattison, J. (1973). Effects of Touch on Self-exploration and the Therapeutic Relationship. *Journal of Consulting and Clinical Psychology, 40*, 170-175.

Perez, M.I. (1991). Communication Competence: Nonverbal and Paralinguistic Classroom Interactions among Teachers and Students with and without Migratory Experience in the United States. Paper Based on Doctoral Dissertation.

Pogrebin, L.C. (1987). *Among friends*. New York, NY: McGraw-Hill Book Co.

Poyatos, F. (Ed.) (1988). *Cross-cultural Perspectives in Nonverbal Communication*.

Lewiston, NY: C.J. Hogrefe Press.

Reischauer, E.O. (1977). *The Japanese*. Cambridge, MA: The Belknap Press of Harvard University Press.

Remland, M.S. & Jones, T.S. (1988). Cultural and Sex Differences in Touch Avoidance. *Perceptual and Motor Skills, 67*, 544-546.

Richmond, V., McCroskey, J.C. & Payne, S.K. (1991). *Nonverbal Behavior in Interpersonal Relations*. Englewood Cliffs, NJ: Prentice Hall.

Rosenfeld, L.B., Kartus, S. & Ray, C. (1976). Body Accessibility Revisited. *Journal of Communication*, 27-30.

Silberman, B.S. (1962). *Japan and Korea: a Critical Bibliography* Tucson, AZ: The University of Arizona Press.

Spitz, R.A. (1945). Hospitalism. An Inquiry into the Genesis of Psychiatric Conditions in early Childhood. In O. Fenichel (Ed.), *The Psychoanalytical Study of the Child, 1*, 53-74.

Stier, D.S. & Hall, J.A. (1984). Gender Differences in Touch: an Empirical and Theoretical Review. *Journal of Personality and Social Psychology, 47*, 440-459.

Thayer, S.T. (1986). History and Strategies of Research on Social Touch. *Journal of Nonverbal Behavior, 10*, 12-28.

Thayer, S.T. (1988, March). Encounters. *Psychology Today*, 31-36.

Werner, O. & Campbell, D. (1970). Translating, Working through Interpreters and Problems of Decentering. In R. Maroll and R. Cohen (Eds.), *A Handbook of Method and Cultural Anthropology*. New York, NY: American Museum of History.

4. WORLD VIEW DIFFERENCES AMONG KOREANS AND AMERICANS*

Myung-Seok Park
Dankook University

Peggy Cooke
Donald W. Klopf
West Virginia University

* Paper prepared for the June 1992 World Communication Association—Korea
Convention, Seoul, Korea

Cultures are distinguishable by various factors. When combined these factors create unique cultural identities. One of the factors is world view, a relatively stable system of beliefs about ontological issues sanctioned by a culture and maintained by its members. These beliefs structure reality, provide a frame of reference, and influence members' perspective of the world. The members' thoughts, feelings, and behaviors are mediated by world view (Dodd, 1982; Klopf, 1991; Pennington, 1985; Samovar, Porter & Jain, 1981).

Gilgen and Cho (1979a) developed a means for studying world view. They created and tested a questionnaire concerned with Eastern and Western cultural world views. The study reported here broadens the work of Gilgen and Cho as it measures the world view of university students in Korea and the United States for comparative purposes. To understand more fully the study's results, the concept of world view is explained in some detail.

WORLD VIEW

World view beliefs address many of the same issues found in religious doctrines. Although world view is not the same as religion, it is greatly influenced by both historical and current religions within a culture (Dodd, 1982). Major religions, such as Confucianism and Christianity, align with and influence distinct, correlated world views and cultures (Dodd, 1982; Kim, 1988; Porter & Samovar, 1991).

World view centers around ontological issues. These concern existence and being, issues of humans, inanimate objects, supernatural powers and deities (Dodd, 1987; Klopf, 1991). Humans try to conceive relational boundaries for themselves, the things around them, and the powers beyond them.

A better understanding of the relational concerns is developed using Kluckhohn and Strodtbeck's (1961) belief orientations. To them, beliefs may cluster along categories or orientations. Important to world view are human nature, relationships between humans and nature, time, activity, and relationships among humans.

The first category or orientation, human nature, questions whether humans are basically good, bad, or a combination of good and bad. Basic human nature defines the potential for human life, as well as for any relationship, whether to self, others, or things.

The second, humans and nature, deals with humans' relationships with nature. Does nature subjugate humans, do humans master nature, or do humans and nature exist in harmony? Humans can consider nature as the immediate surrounding world or the worlds beyond. Humans grapple with the possibility of life beyond this planet while they covet the thought that they are central in the universe.

The third orientation, time, determines which perspective humans hold about their position on an infinite time-line: past, present, or future. Do humans exist merely as a momentary flash in planetary life, or are they tied to all past existence and are hoping for ties to what will be in the future? Do humans live for one time, for one period? Or, do they live on in multiple existences?

The fourth, activity, is about the requirements for human existence. Do people exist simply by being? Does existence require doing? Or, are humans beings-in-becoming, with no absolute point for being?

The final orientation, the relationships among humans, pertains to how people relate to each other. It questions whether people can live independently, as autonomous individuals, or if their existence and identity require association with a group or with historical lineage.

These categories or orientations act as components of a culture's world view. They appear here as universal components, but they can occur in various cultures in different orders and strengths. Each culture has its own world view.

A culture determines world view and perpetuates it in its members through varied cultural institutions (Dodd, 1982; Jain, 1991; Kim, 1991; Klopf, 1991; Roberts, 1979; Sitaram & Cogdell, 1976). World view, like other cultural factors, belongs to the group, but is carried by the individual (Kluckhohn & Strodtbeck, 1961). Institutions such as the family, school, and religion pass on world view beliefs in the process of strengthening cultural uniqueness, cohesion, and historical continuity (Samovar & Porter, 1991). Institutions use various techniques for passing on beliefs such as the world view. Modeling, conditioning, social interaction, and language learning are among them (Epstein, 1970; Kluckhohn, 1951; McCroskey, Richmond, & Stewart, 1986; Roberts, 1979; Rokeach, 1973).

Social scientists have long taken an interest in the relationships between culture and world view--first anthropologists and more recently intercultural communication scholars (Dodd, 1982). The challenge for present-day scientists comes in trying to measure a concept that is conceived, held, and passed on primarily at an implicit level. Although every member of a culture likely abides by the culture's world view, few are cognizant of specific, related beliefs.

Gilgen and Cho (1979a) designed a questionnaire to attempt to measure world view. They held that two distinct perspectives could organize cultures: Eastern and Western. Their questionnaire aimed to differentiate cultures and world views according to these two dichotomous perspectives.

The Eastern perspective was born out of the major Eastern religions of Buddhism, Taoism, Confucianism, and Hinduism. An overriding characteristic of all of these was monism, a tendency to seek a life of oneness and wholeness. The Western perspective was born out of the Judeo-Christian traditions, which promote duality and choosing between opposites.

Gilgen and Cho (1979a) offered specific beliefs for consideration in contrasting the Eastern and Western perspectives.

The Eastern perspective included:

1. Human beings are one with nature
2. Human beings perceive the spiritual and physical as one.
3. Human beings perceive the mind and body as one.
4. Human beings should accept the basic oneness with nature rather than try to label, categorize, manipulate, control, analyze, orconsume worldly things.
5. Human beings should feel comfortable with anyone because of

their oneness with all existence.

6. Science and technology create an illusion of progress at best.

7. Enlightenment, a state where all differences disappear, means to achieve oneness with the universe.

8. Enlightenment is achieved through meditation.

The Western perspective included these beliefs:

1. Human beings have characteristics that distinguish them from nature and the spiritual.

2. Human beings consist of body, mind, and spirit.

3. Human beings are overshadowed by the existence of a personal God.

4. Human beings must manipulate and control nature to survive.

5. Human beings must think rationally and analytically.

6. The good life and hope for its future continuation is found in science and technology.

7. Human beings should reward actions and the competitive spirit.

Gilgen and Cho (1979a) developed their questionnaire based on these dichotomous beliefs. They created paired statements (East-West) for an assortment of issues related to the beliefs and categorized them into five orientations: Man and the spiritual, Man and nature, Man and society, Man and himself, and the rationality of Man.

MEASURING EASTERN AND WESTERN THOUGHT

The measure consists of 34 pairs of items arranged in random order. The resulting 68 items are rated on a Likert-type scale, from agree strongly ("1") to strongly disagree ("5"). The Gilgen and Cho scoring method assigns a weight of 2 to items marked "strongly agree," a weight of 1 to "agree" items, and a weight of 0 to "have no opinion," "disagree" and "disagree strongly." The "0" weights make possible a scale ranging from 0 to 100. An "Eastern Tendency" is defined as a score greater than 50; a "Western Tendency" as a score less than 50 (Gilgen and Cho, 1979a).

In their development and testing (Gilgen & Cho, 1979a, 1979b, 1980; Gilgen, Cho, & Stensrud, 1980; Cho & Gilgen, 1980), the initial test-retest reliability was 0.75 (Pearson correlation). They noted that as "adequate test-retest reliability at least for college students" (Gilgen & Cho, 1979a, p. 839). Compton's (1983) study resulted in a coefficient alpha (Cronbach, 1951) of 0.70. These tests occurred within cultures, except for one cross-cultural study (Gilgen & Cho, 1980).

The literature on world view suggests that every culture has a unique world view created through the ordering of beliefs in a hierarchical system and the Gilgen and Cho (1979a) questionnaire provides a means for studying world view across cultures.

METHODS

University students from Korea and the United States, representing a cross-section of academic disciplines, participated in this study of world view. The respondents included 160 (110 men and 50 women) Dankook University, Seoul, Korea, students and 190 (84 men, 106 women) West Virginia University, Morgantown, U.S.A., students. The mean age of the Koreans was 21.9 years and the Americans 23.0 years—a significant difference but analysis showed this difference had no impact on the results.

Each respondent completed the Gilgen and Cho (1979a) Questionnaire to Measure Eastern and Western Thought in English, the language of the measure. The Korean students were versed in the English language and were capable of comprehending the measure's terminology. The completed questionnaires were scored and then analyzed through a *t*-test comparison of the two cultures.

RESULTS/DISCUSSION

The results of the analysis show a significant difference between the Koreans (M = 54.67, SD = 7.51) and the Americans (M = 45.00, SD = 10.82; t = 8.19; p < .0001). Nonsignificant effects were found for gender and age.

Gilgen and Cho (1979a) defined an Eastern tendency as a mean greater than 50 and the Korean respondents with a mean score of over 54 obviously reflect an Eastern world view. A Western tendency is a mean less than 50 and with a mean score of 45, the Americans observe a Western world view. The results confirm Korea's place among cultures with Eastern tendencies following a collectivistic relational nature. Other Oriental cultures including Japan and the People's Republic of China are collectivisms, and Japan, its world view also examined (Cooke, 1992), represents the Eastern world view perspective as well. The results indicate the dualistic nature of the American culture with its allegiance to a Western world view and an individualistic relational nature. Koreans, therefore, would be expected to believe that humans are one with nature with the spiritual and physical as one. Americans, in contrast, would be expected to believe that humans have qualities that separate them from nature and the spiritual, that they are not one with nature.

Korean communication practices exhibit world view beliefs of a collectivistic culture. Ideally, Koreans strive to uphold harmony through their communication. Koreans attend to relationships first, then subject matter, using honorifics to indicate respect for others and modesty about self (Crane, 1967; Seonghong, 1983; Park, 1979). Although Koreans allow for selfhood, individualism does not prevail. Crane (1967) and Park (1979) note that Koreans speak to enhance one another's self respect while encouraging group conformity. Korean language stresses the importance of the group, family, and harmony, and Confucian righteousness is a influencing factor (Park, 1979).

American communication practices display world view beliefs of an individualistic culture. Americans place a high premium on the values of individualism and self-reliance (Althen, 1988), and usually do not seek deep involvement with other people. They most likely will avoid such involvement, perceiving it as a threat to their independence and freedom of action. Americans do not seek the sort of deep, mutual interdependence typical of communicative relationships among Koreans. While the "we" is important in Korea, Americans are concerned about the "I" — the difference between the collectivism of Korea and the individualism of the United States.

The concept of world view merits additional study among Koreans especially as Koreans are compared to other cultures. World view is a unique identifier of cultural characteristics, and in a world where modern transportation and communication facilities make intercultural contact a reality, any means of improving knowledge about world cultures should help in eliminating misunderstandings in intercultural contacts.

WORLD VIEW QUESTIONNAIRE

Please respond to the following statements by writing the number that best represents your agreement or disagreement (for each statement) on the lines to the left of the statements:

1..... I agree strongly
2..... I agree, but with some reservations
3..... I have no opinion
4..... I disagree, but only moderately
5..... I disagree strongly

Number   Statement

_____ 1. A high level of consumption, even if it means some waste, is essential to a strong economy and a high standard of living.

_____ 2. A meaningful life depends more on learning to cooperate than learning to compete.

_____ 3. I love to sit quietly just watching the clouds or a wild flower.

_____ 4. Man should strive to return to nature.

_____ 5. Inaction makes me very nervous and uncomfortable.

_____ 6. The only real progress man has achieved has been through science and technology.

_____ 7. Complex problems cannot be understood by breaking them into smaller components and then analyzing each component.

_____ 8. Suffering, while painful and unpleasant, is basically a positive experience.

_____ 9. The main purpose of learning is to be able to get a good job.

——— 10. Suffering should be avoided at all cost because it destroys the meaning of life.

——— 11. Meditation properly practiced can be a rich source of personal enlightenment; even when practiced by amateurs it may offer a way to relax.

——— 12. I feel that my dreams are an integral part of me.

——— 13. Money frees us from drudgery and meaningless work.

——— 14. The ideal society is one in which each person by working individually for his own goals benefits everyone.

——— 15. I enjoy being by myself in the dark.

——— 16. While plants and animals are essential to human existence, I have no personal bond with most of them.

——— 17. Man should try to harmonize with nature rather than manipulate and control it.

——— 18. I cannot honestly say that it bothers me very much to step on an ant or bee deliberately.

——— 19. Heart and kidney transplants are natural and wonderful medical advances.

——— 20. Science and technology have provided man with anillusion of progress; an illusion he will later pay for dearly.

——— 21. Probably some useful information about people can be acquired through questionnaires.

——— 22. It is primarily through thinking and classifying that our experiences take on meaning.

——— 23. Suicide is just plain wrong.

——— 24. True learning is directed toward self-understanding.

——— 25. I enjoy eating by myself in a restaurant.

——— 26. One of the most important things you can teach your children is how to compete successfully in the world.

_____ 27. The ideal society is one in which each person subordinates his or her own desires and works consciously for the good of the community.

_____ 28. Money tends to enslave people.

_____ 29. I feel ill at ease by myself in strange places.

_____ 30. I feel a real sense of kinship with most plants and animals.

_____ 31. If there is a soul, I believe that after I die it will lose its individuality and become one with the overall spirituality of the universe.

_____ 32. Science is our main hope for the future.

_____ 33. Language gives form and meaning to our experiences.

_____ 34. The use of artificial kidneys and plastic hearts is going too far; it is unnatural.

_____ 35. Anxiety usually results in personal growth.

_____ 36. Knowing that we shall die gives meaning to life.

_____ 37. Anxiety usually leads to unproductive and even self destructive behavior.

_____ 38. Meditation is at best a form of relaxation and at worst a dangerous escape from reality and our responsibilities.

_____ 39. Death really doesn't make much sense to me.

_____ 40. I find most strangers interesting and easy to get to know.

_____ 41. The deep inner realm of man is basically primitive and evil.

_____ 42. People should have the opportunity to work themselves out of the situation in life they are born into.

_____ 43. It is within his deep inner self that man will find true enlightenment.

_____ 44. Material possessions are for me a deep source of satisfaction.

_____ 45. A new idea should be treasured whether it is useful or not.

_____ 46. Administering questionnaires is not a very effectiveway to find out about people.

_____ 47. Thoughts tend to isolate us from our feelings.

_____ 48. Only ideas that help us do something better have much value.

_____ 49. Suicide is sometimes a noble and natural choice.

_____ 50. I feel awkward and self-conscious with most strangers.

_____ 51. The world keeps passing through cycles, over and over again, never really changing.

_____ 52. I like to travel alone sometimes to new places.

_____ 53. Man is moving by some grand plan toward an hisorical goal.

_____ 54. I believe in a personal god to whom I must account after death.

_____ 55. Language tends to interfere with our ability to experience things naturally and fully.

_____ 56. My dreams seem like an alien part of me.

_____ 57. People should accept the role in life they are given by their parents' status in society.

_____ 58. We should only consume what we actually need.

_____ 59. Man's progress has resulted primarily from his abil-ity, through science and technology, to control andmodify the natural world.

_____ 60. I do not believe in a personal god.

_____ 61. Science is a destructive force in the long run.

_____ 62. The best way to understand something is to subdivide it into smaller components and analyze each component carefully.

_____ 63. I cannot stand eating by myself.

_____ 64. I hate to kill anything, even insects.

_____ 65. Man should strive to free himself from the uncompromising forces of nature.

_____   66. I am usually afraid when I find myself alone in a dark place.

_____   67. I get very little pleasure from material possessions.

_____   68. I believe in a personal soul which will continue to exist after death.

Please complete these questions:

AGE _____   SEX: Femal _____   Male _____

YEAR IN SCHOOL _____

Thank you for participating in this study.

REFERENCES

Althen, G. (1988). *American Ways.* Yarmouth, ME.: Intercultural Press.

Cho, J.H. & Gilgen, A.R. (1980). Performance of Korean Medical and Nursing Students on the East-West Questionnaire. *Psychological Reports , 47,* 1093-1094.

Compton, W.C. (1983). On the Validity of the East-West Questionnaire. *Psychological Reports, 52,* 117-118.

Cooke, Peggy A. (1992). *Perceptions of World View among American, Japanese, Korean, and Puerto Rican University Students.* M.A. Thesis, West Virginia University.

Crane, P.S. (1967). *Korean Patterns,* Seoul: Hollym.

Cronbach, L.J. (1951). Coefficient Alpha and the Internal Structure of Tests. *Psychometrika, 16,* 297-334.

Dodd, C.H. (1982). *Dynamics of Intercultural Communication.* Dubuque, IA: Wm. C. Brown Company.

Dodd, C.H. (1987). *Dynamics of Intercultural Communication* (2nd ed.). Dubuque, IA: Wm. C. Brown Company.

Epstein, E.H. (1970). *Politics and Education in Puerto Rico: Documentary Survey of the Language Issue.* Metuchen, NJ: The Scarecrow Press, Inc.

Gilgen, A.R. & Cho, J.H. (1979a). Questionnaire to Measure Eastern and Western Thought. *Psychological Reports, 44,* 835-841.

Gilgen, A.R. & Cho, J.H. (1979b). Performance of Eastern and Western Oriented College Students on the Value Survey and Ways of Life Scale. *Psychological Reports, 45,* 263-268.

Gilgen, A.R. & Cho, J.H. (1980). Comparison of Performance on the East-West Questionnaire, Zen Scale, and Consciousness I, II, and III Scales. *Psychological Reports, 47,* 583-588.

Gilgen, A.R., Cho, J.H., & Stensrud, R. (1980). Eastern and Western Perspectives in Transpersonal Belief Systems. *Psychological Reports, 47,* 1344-1346.

Jain, N.C. (1991). World View and Cultural Patterns of India. In L.A. Samovar & R.E. Porter (Eds.), *Intercultural Communication: A Reader* (6th ed.) (pp.78-87). Belmont, CA: Wadsworth.

Kim, Y.Y. (1988). Intercultural Personhood: An Integration of Eastern and Western Perspectives. In L.A. Samovar & R.E. Porter (Eds.), *Intercultural Communication: A Reader* (5th ed.) (pp.401-411). Belmont, CA: Wadsworth.

Kim, Y.Y. (1991). Communication and Cross-cultural Adaptation. In L.A. Samovar & R.E. Porter (Eds.), *Intercultural Communication: A Reader* (6th ed.) (pp.383-390). Belmont, CA: Wadsworth.

Klopf, D.W. (1991). *Intercultural Encounters.* Englewood, CA: Morton.

Kluckhohn, C. (1951). Values and Value-Orientations in the Theory of Action. In T. Parsons & E.A. Shils (Eds.), *Toward a General Theory of Action* (pp. 388-433). Cambridge, MA: Harvard University Press.

Kluckhohn, F.R. & Strodtbeck, F.L. (1961). *Variations in Value Orientations.* Evanston, IL: Row, Peterson and Company.

McCroskey, J.C., Richmond, V.R., & Stewart, R.A. (1986). *One on One: The Foundations of Interpersonal Communication.* Englewood Cliffs, NJ: Prentice-Hall.

Park, M-S (1979). *Communication Styles in Two Different Cultures: Korean and American.* Seoul, Han Shin.

Pennington, D.L. (1985). Intercultural Communication. In L.A. Samovar & R.E. Porter (Eds.), *Intercultural Communication: A Reader* (4th ed.). Belmont, CA: Wadsworth.

Porter, R.E. & Samovar, L.A. (1991). Basic Principles of Intercultural Communication. In L.A. Samovar & R.E. Porter (Eds.), *Intercultural Communication: A Reader* (6th ed.) (pp.522). Belmont, CA: Wadsworth.

Roberts, G.O. (1979). Terramedian Value Systems and Their Significance. In M.K. Asante, E. Newmark, & C.A. Blake (Eds.), *Handbook of Intercultural Communication.* Beverly Hills, CA: Sage.

Rokeach, M. (1973). *The Nature of Human Values.* New York: Free Press.

Samovar, L.A. & Porter, R.E. (1991). *Intercultural Communication: A Reader* (6th ed.). Belmont, CA: Wadsworth.

Samovar, L.A., Porter, R.E., & Jain, N.C. (1981). *Understanding Intercultural Communication.* Belmont, CA: Wadsworth.

Seonghong, Min (1983). Communication Styles in Two Different Cultures: Korean and Japan. In M-S Park (ed.), *Cross-Cultural Perspectives on Communication Encounters and Conflicts.* Proceedings of the 1983 CAP-Korea International Convention on Cross-Cultural Communication: Encounters and Conflicts, July 28-31, Seoul, Korea.

Sitaram, K.S. & Cogdell, R. (1976). *Foundations of Intercultural Communication.* Columbus: Charles Merrill.

5. KOREAN AND AMERICAN SELF-MONITORING PERCEPTIONS*

Myung-Seok Park
Dankook University

Trace T. Lang
West Virginia University

Donald W. Klopf
West Virginia University

* Paper prepared for the June 1992 World Communication Association – Korea
Convention, Seoul, Korea

ABSTRACT

This inquiry compared differences in self-monitoring between Korean and American subjects. The study involved the examination of the self-reports of 191 Korean subjects and 102 American subjects. Results of the survey indicate no significant disparity between Korean and American subjects. Unexpectedly, Korean females reported significantly lower levels of self-monitoring than the other cell groups. Explanations and implications of these findings are discussed.

KOREAN AND AMERICAN SELF-MONITORING PERCEPTIONS

Communicative competence partially results from a communicator's ability to be sensitive to the communication situation and to be flexible in response to it (Pierson & Nelson, 1991). This sensitivity is a personality disposition that governs appropriateness of behavior (Schneider, 1988) and is identified by Snyder (1974) as self-monitoring.

Self-monitoring is examined in this report cross-culturally, specifically comparing Korean and American university students' self-monitoring abilities in perceived communication settings. The theoretical impetus behind the examination is to determine what self-monitoring differences, if any, occur between Koreans and Americans.

SELF-MONITORING

Self-monitoring is a construct related to awareness that was developed by Snyder (1974). He believed individuals differ in the extent to which they monitor (observe and regulate or control) their expressive behavior and self-presentation. Some have a proclivity for monitoring a communicative environment effectively. They can home in on cues that inform them as to the appropriate communicative behavior in that environment. Observing a particular communicative situation, they know what behavior is suitable in that situation and act accordingly (Spitzberg & Cupach, 1984). For example, confronting a person who has lost a loved one, they will be sensitive to the person's loss and will be able to express feelings of condolence. Meeting an angry co-worker, they will know how to diffuse the anger and yet be able to sympathize with the individual's vexation. These people are called high self-monitors.

High self-monitors are attentive, other-oriented, and adaptable to diverse communication situations. They possess the ability to effectively manage the impressions of other persons by presenting themselves in desired ways (Spitzberg & Cupach, 1984). They are good at learning socially acceptable behavior, possess good emotional self-control, and can create what ever effects they want. They are able to intentionally express and communicate emotion both in voice and through facial expressions. They will seek the necessary information needed to compare themselves with their peers (Snyder, 1974).

High self-monitors are attentive to social information (Berscheid, Graziano, Monson, & dermer, 1976), seek out information about others (Elliot, 1979), are knowledgeable about how others behave in social situations (Snyder & Cantor, 1979), show varied emotional responses (Lippa, 1976; Snyder, 1974), choose work partners on the basis of situational demands (Snyder, Gangestad, & Simpson, 1983), and provide situational explanations for their behavior (Snyder, 1976). Their behavior tends to vary from situation to situation as they adapt to each situation's demands (Bem & Allen, 1974; Snyder & Monson, 1975). High self-monitors are prone to initiating conversations (Ickes & Barnes, 1977), speak for short periods, and are apt to interrupt other speakers (Dabbs, Evans, Hopper, & Purvis, 1980). In self-disclosing situations, they are likely to reciprocate the intimacy, emotionality, and descriptive nature of a partner's self-disclosure (Shaffer, Smith & Tomarelli, 1982).

Low self-monitors behave in contrary fashion to that of the high self-monitors. They pay less attention to situational cues and have little concern for the appropriateness of their communicative behavior

(Schneider, 1988). They attend less than high self-monitors to the expressions of others and monitor and control their behavior less. Their communication seems internal-controlled from within — rather than situational or interpersonal specifications of appropriateness (Snyder, 1974). But they show more consistency across situations than high self-monitors and their behavior is better predicted by their personal qualities. Thus, a low self-monitor who behaviorally is dominant will be dominant in all situations, not adjusting and adapting to situational demands as a high self-monitor would (Schneider, 1988).

Low self-monitors prefer homogeneous and undifferentiated social environments, choosing to spend time with friends who hold likes and dislikes similar to theirs (Cody & McLaughlin, 1985). They are less expressive than high self-monitors, less skilled at employing strategies of social influence, and more internally (dispositionally) guided in their behavior (Miller, deTurck, & Kalbfleisch, 1983; Cody, Smith, Lee, & Greene, 1986).

CROSS-CULTURAL IMPLICATIONS

Considering that the self-monitoring construct delineates two divergent communication orientations (low self-monitors who are internal and dispositional and high self-monitors, external and situational), the expectation would seem natural to find culturally-based propensities toward one orientation or the other. However, little cross-cultural research exists on self-monitoring. Only a paucity of studies have examined its role and prevalence in dissimilar cultures (Gudykunst, 1981; Gudykunst & Nishida, 1984; Gudykunst, 1985).

Conceivably, the most extreme cross-cultural disparity in self-monitoring should exist between cultures located at opposite ends of what has come to be known as the high-context/low-context dimension or continuum. Hall (1976) categorized cultures as either high-or low-context. But context is really a cultural dimension that ranges from high to low (Samovar & Porter, 1991). In high-context cultures, most of the information lies either in the physical context or within the people who are part of the interaction. Little information is in the coded, verbal message. In low-context cultures, the verbal message contains most of the information and very little is embedded within the context or the individuals. Intuitively, the probability that the utility of self-monitoring skills would be fostered and perpetuated in high-context cultures, those that extract a disportionate amount of meaning and communicative behavior from the physical context, would be high. High self-monitors should abound in high-context cultures, it could be predicted. Likewise, the expectation should be that low self-monitors would characterize people in low-context cultures, where people speak their minds often regardless of the situation. Generally, East Asian cultures would be classed as high-context and Western cultures as low-context. Persons living in high-context cultures ought to be high self-monitors and those living in low-context cultures presumably would be low-self-monitors.

Additionally, the collectivistic/individualistic dimension should be a consideration in self-monitoring. Typical members of collectivist cultures concentrate their interpersonal efforts on developing, maintaining, and enhancing group goals and relationships. They are concerned with the socially perceived correctness or appropriateness of their behavior. East Asian cultures tend to be collectivistic. Conversely, the average members of individualistic cultures value the pursuit of individual goals and nonconformity in the form of the uniqueness or differentness of their self-expression. Equalitarianism is stressed, and the people are prone to join many groups, but their personal goals take precedence over those of the group. Interactional conflict is thought beneficial. Disagreements in social relationships help clear the air and supposedly lead to more fruitful encounters. In collectivistic cultures, harmony in interpersonal relationships is the goal (Klopf & Thomson, 1992). Western cultures tend to be individualistic. High self-monitoring would appear to be appropriate in the collectivistic cultures and low self-monitoring in the individualistic.

RATIONALE AND HYPOTHESIS

Given these characteristics of East Asian and Western cultures, a logical prediction for self-monitoring differences is that Asian cultures exhibit higher incidences of self-monitoring than the Western cultures. In previous studies, however, this prediction received no support. For example, Gudykunst and Nishida (1984) discovered no significant differences between the Japanese and American samples with respect to self-monitoring. They attempted to explain this lack of difference by positing that a generational gap between the Japanese students who constituted the Japanese sample and their ancestry may be signaling a possible trend toward Japanese individualism — a trend mirroring Western cultures. More likely, their results reflect the natural tendencies of young people who are away at school to exhibit individualistic feelings. Once settled into employment and their own family life, the collectivistic tendencies will reassert themselves.

The theoretical underpinnings for the current investigation revolve around assessing whether there are true self-monitoring differences between Koreans who are members of high-context, collectivistic cultures and Americans who are members of low-context, individualistic cultures. The hypothesis guiding this investigation is that Korean subjects (university students) will report higher levels of self-monitoring traits than American subjects (university students).

METHODS

The subjects included 191 (116 men, 75 women) Dankook University students in Seoul, Korea, and 102 (49 men, 53 women) West Virginia University students in Morgantown, United States. No significant difference in age or year in school was found for the two groups.

The Snyder (1974) Self-Monitoring of Expressive Behavior scale was administered to the subjects. Since the Koreans were conversant in the English language, the language of the scale, its translation was unnecessary and the English version was used for both groups.

The scale consists of twenty-five true-false self-descriptive statements which describe (a) concern with the social appropriateness of one's self-presentation (e.g., "At parties and social gatherings, I do not attempt to do or say things that others will like"); (b) attention to social comparison information as cues to appropriate self-expression (e.g., "When I am uncertain how to act in social situations, I look to the behavior of others for cues"); (c) the ability to control and modify one's self-presentation and expressive behavior (e.g., "I can look anyone in the eye and tell a lie, if for the right end"); (d) the use of this ability in certain situations (e.g., "I may deceive people by being friendly when I really dislike them"); and (e) the extent to which the respondent's behavior and self-presentation is cross-situationally consistent or variant (e.g., "In different situations and with different people, I often act like very different persons").

RESULTS AND DISCUSSION

To determine differences in self-monitoring between the Koreans and Americans, an analysis of variance was conducted with two dimensions of culture (Koreans and Americans) and of gender (men and women). The hypothesis was not supported. The Korean subjects did not report higher levels of self-monitoring than did American subjects. No significant effect was found for culture and gender, and no significant interaction was found between culture and gender.

A t-test post hoc analysis of mean scores revealed significantly lower levels of self-monitoring for Korean women ($M=11.70$, $SD=3.83$) than Korean men ($M=12.39$, $SD=3.62$; $t=2.24$, $p < .05$). However, no significant difference was discovered between Korean women and American women ($M=12.45$, $SD=3.75$), between Korean women and American men ($M=12.47$, $SD=4.32$), between Korean men and American women, between Korean men and American men, and between American men and women.

The combined mean for both Korean and American groups (M=12.09, SD =3.85) with a median of 12.00 and a mode of 13.00 registered almost at the midpoint of all possible scores-0 to 25-indicating that as a totality the Korean and American participants reported modest levels of self-monitoring aptitude.

A t-test analysis confirmed the analysis of variance finding that neither group differed significantly from each other. The total Korean group (M=11.91, SD= 3.74) was not significantly different than the American group (M=12.40, SD=4.05).

The results of this investigation conform to the earlier studies (Gudykunst and Nishida, 1984) that detected minimal self-monitoring differences between East Asian and American subjects. Although the expectation is that persons in high-context, collectivistic cultures should perceive themselves as being adaptable and can adjust to the circumstances of specific communication situations, the results of this and the other studies prove otherwise.

The reasons are likely manifold. The Snyder (1974) Self-Monitoring of Expressive Behavior scale, used in all of the studies, might be at fault. A different scale possibly would provide different and perhaps more accurate results. A more pertinent reason has to do with the subjects. The scale measures rather sophisticated awareness and adaptation skills reflective of sensitive and knowledgeable individuals. The subjects in this study and the others were university students, undergraduates and lower classmen for the most part who quite possibly have not well developed self-monitoring skills and would not be so perceptive about social comparison information dealing with appropriate patterns of expression and experience. These subjects probably have not learned a concern for suitability of their self-presentation. Such interpersonal competence comes from an understanding of what is a culture's normative communication behavior — an understanding often enhanced through university communication courses. Additionally, such competence comes from years of trial and error practice in true life situations. University students may not have the degree of experience necessary to effectively function in all communication interactions. This is not to say that the students are not emotionally expressive or even that they are less so than those who are able to monitor their presentations. Rather, the students self-presentational and expressive behavior may seem, in a functional sense, to be controlled from within by their affective states — they express themselves as they feel — rather than monitored, controlled, and molded to fit the situation as self-monitors would function. This reason, similar to the one advanced by Snyder (1974) seems a more logical explanation for the results than that suggested by Gudykunst and Nishida (1984) who felt that the Japanese were becoming more individualistic in nature.

REFERENCES

Bem, D. J., & Allen, A. (1974). On Predicting Some of the People Some of the Time: The Search for Cross-situational Consistencies in Behavior. *Psychological Review*, 81, 506–520.

Briggs, S. R., Cheek, J. M., & Buss, A. H. (1980). An Analysis of Self-monitoring Scale. *Journal of Personality and Social Psychology, 38,* 679-686.

Bercheid, E., Graziano, W., Monson, T., & Dermer, M. (1976). Outcome Dependency: Attention, Attribution and Attraction. *Journal of Personality and Social Psychology, 34,* 978-989.

Cody, M. J., Smith, S. W., Lee, W. S., & Greene, J. O. (1986, November). Self-Monitoring, Gender, and the Social Influence Process. Paper presented to the annual meeting of the Speech Communication Association, Chicago.

Cody, M. J., & McLaughlin, M. L. (1985). The Situation as a Construct in Interpersonal Communication Research. In M. L. Knapp & G. R. Miller (Eds.). *Handbook of Interpersonal Communication*. Beverly Hills, CA: Sage.

Dabbs, J. M. Jr., Evans, M. S., Hopper, C. H., & Purvis, J. A. (1980). Self-Monitors in Conversations: What do they monitor? *Journal of Personality and Social Psychology, 39,* 278-284.

Elliot, G. C. (1979). Some Effects of Deception and Level of Self-Monitoring on Planning and Reacting to a Self-Presentation. *Journal of Experimental Social Psychology, 15,* 330-342.

Gudykunst, W. B. (1981). Cross-Cultural Comparisons. In C. R. Berger & S. H. Chaffee (Eds.), *Handbook of Communication Science.* (pp. 847-889).

Gudykunst, W. B., & Nishida, T. (1984). Individual and Cultural Influences on Uncertainty Reduction. *Communication Monographs, 51,* 23-36.

Gudykunst, W. B. (1985). The Influence of Cultural Selectivity, Type of Relationship, and Self-Monitoring on Uncertainty Reduction Processes. *Communication Monographs, 52,* 203-217.

Hall, E. T. (1976). *Beyond Culture*. Garden City, NY: Doubleday.

Ickes, D. W., & Barnes, R. D. (1977). The Role of Sex and Self-Monitoring in Unstructured Dyadic Interactions. *Journal of Personality and Social Psychology, 35,* 315-330.

Klopf, D. W., & Thompson, C. A. (1992). *Communication in the Multicultural Classroom*. Minneapolis: Burgess.

Lipps, R. (1976). Expressive Control and the Leakage of Dispositional Introversion-Extroversion during Role-Playing Teaching. *Journal of Personality, 44,* 541-559.

Miller, G. R., deTurck, M. A., & Kalbfleisch, P. J. (1983). Self-Monitoring, Rehearsal, and Deceptive Communication. *Human Communication Research. 10,* 97-118.

Pearson, J. C., & Nelson, P. E. (1991). *Understanding and Sharing: An Introduction to Speech Communication*. Fifth ed. Dubuque, Iowa: William C. Brown.

Samovar, C. A., & Porter, R. E. (1991). *Communication Between Cultures*. Belmont, CA: Wadsworth.

Schneider, D. J. (1988). *Introduction to Social Psychology.* San Diego: Harcourt, Bruce Jovanovich.

Spitzberg, B. H., & Cupach, W. R. (1984). *Interpersonal Communication Competence.* Beverly Hills, CA: Sage.

Snyder, M. (1974). Self-Monitoring of Expressive Behavior. *Journal of Personality and Social Psychology, 12,* 526-537.

Snyder, M .(1979). Self-Monitoring processes. In L. Berkowitz(Ed.), *Advances in Experimental Social Psychology, 12,* 85-128.

Snyder, M., & Cantor, N. (1979). Testing Hypotheses about Other People: The Use of Historical Knowledge. *Journal of Experimental Social Psychology, 15,* 330-342.

Snyder, M., Gangstad, S., & Simpson, J. A. (1983). Choosing friends as activity Partners: The Role of Self-Monitoring. *Journal of Personality and Social Psychology, 45,* 1061-1072.

Snyder, M. (1976). Attribution and Behavior: Social Perception and Social Causation. In J. H. Harvey, W. J. Ickes, & R. F. Kidd (Eds.), *New Directions in Attribution Research.,* (Vol 1), Hillsdale, NJ: Lawrence Erlbaum.

Snyder, M., & Monson, T. C. (1975). Persons, Situations, and the Control of Social Behavior. *Journal of Personality and Social Psychology, 32,* 637-644.

6. COMPARING HUMAN VALUES IN KOREA AND THE UNITED STATES*

Myung-Seok Park
Dankook University

Candice Thomas
West Virginia University

Donald W. Klopf
West Virginia University

* Paper prepared for the annual conference of the World Communication—Korea Association 1993

Human communicative behavior is heavily influenced by a complex system of needs, values, beliefs, and attitudes, a system called the personal orientation system. The system activates and directs human behavior in communication situations as it helps determine a person's relationships to the ideas being discussed and the people discussing them. The system tells a person what is right or wrong, good or bad, unimportant or important, and largely controls the person's everyday behavior (Klopf, 1991).

The needs, values, beliefs, and attitudes that make up the system are learned, and they are learned in a framework imposed by a specific culture. The four components of the system are culturally imposed, and they will vary from culture to culture.

Of the four, the concern in this paper is with values, the evaluative and judgmental aspect of the personal orientation system. They function as the governing reference for human needs, and guide and direct human behavior. Rising out of the culture, values make known to the members of a culture what is important and satisfactory and what is not, determining for the culture what should be done and what should not. They are the guidelines specifying what is proper behavior and what is not. Thus values help determine a person's behavior in communication settings by functioning as criteria for judgment and choice in the course of action (Ishii & Klopf, 1989).

The values held by one culture are apt to differ from the values of another. This fact underlies the study of values for communication theorists and speakers. To speak competently across cultures, the values of the cultures should be known.

The purpose of this paper is to examine how persons representing disparate cultures (Korea and the United States) react value-wise to specific communication situations, seeking to discover what value differences, if any, exist between the two cultures.

Values prove to be vital to human communication because of their nature. Once an individual has decided to take action of some sort, the person's values come into play, determining for the individual whether the action contemplated is good or bad, right or wrong.

What a person says will be conditioned by his or her value system. If the person's values allow the use of profanity, the individual probably will mouth obscenities, believing them to be acceptable behavior. If the person is of moral rectitude, the individual's value system will likely not allow the use of wicked, vicious, base, vile, and foul language.

A particular value, however, can differ for a person over time or in differing situations. It can differ in terms of salience, direction, or degree. The highly moral person, not prone to use profanity, might in an exasperating situation, causing bitter vexation and inflaming anger, to employ curses to show chagrin, laying aside his or her normal uprightness. The same holds true for a culture. War may be deplored, but when extremely hostile conditions occur, the culture may resort to battle to defend itself. However, a number of cultures perceive hostility as important in their interactions with members of other cultures. These cultures consider hostility as positive; most consider it negative. The point is that what one culture deems vital, another may not. Values, hence, may vary from culture to culture.

METHOD

To discover if values differ across culture and, if they do, how they do, the Value Preference questionnaire was administered to 174 American university students (males 81, females 93, mean age 21.3 years) and 196 Korean university students (males 96, females 100, mean age 22.1 years) significantly older than the Americans.

The Value Preference questionnaire, being tested in this study as a means of understanding value preferences in situational experiences, has a reliability of .190, low and indicative of a need for further development. The questionnaire confronts respondents with ten dilemma-posing situations (see Table 1). Each situation offers three behavior alternatives, the one chosen suggesting a particular value or value salience. To resolve each dilemma, the respondents choose one of the alternatives, picking the one they feel is most desirable in the circumstances. The one selected indicates the respondent's value preference or the salience it has for that individual.

The ten situations represent different values. These are: first, consideration of the elderly; second, morality; third, emotional display; fourth, equality; fifth, well-being of others; sixth, work relationships; seventh, group centeredness; eighth, honesty; ninth, respect for parent; and tenth, respect for family.

Created in English, since the Korean respondents were English-capable, they completed the English version.

RESULTS

Table 1 presents the results in percentages and notes the results of *t*-test analyses for the American and Korean respondents.

Situation-by-situation, the table shows the majority of both cultures selected alternative *one* for situations four and eight, alternative *two* for situations two and three, and alternative *three* for situations one, six, seven, and nine. On situation five, the Americans were split between alternatives *one* and *two* and on situation ten, the American majority favored alternative *three*. The Koreans differed with the Americans on those two situations, picking *two* in each case.

On situations one, five, nine, and ten, the American and Korean respondents, *t*-test analysis revealed, were significantly different. In situation one, the Americans more strongly preferred the seventy-year old alternative while the Korean minority chose the 45-year old one, causing the difference between the cultures.

Situation five indicates a split between the respondents on the three alternatives, causing the difference. More Americans were inclined to ignore the person lying in the gutter, while the larger number of Koreans wanted to give the help required. However, both American and Korean majorities chose either alternative *two* or *three*, each implying help of some sort for the gutter-lying person.

In situation nine, the difference between the two cultures was significant also, with the largest number of the Koreans inclined to obey their parents and with the American largely wanting to compromise, not holding a wild party but having friends over. Only a small minority of both cultures felt the party should be arranged.

In situation ten, with the two groups significantly different, the American majority desired to go with the friends and the parents alternative, and the larger number of Koreans wanting to go only with their friends. Only small percentages of the respondents felt that they should respect their relatives and family and only attend the family reunion.

DISCUSSION

Several variations are noteworthy. In situation one, in which respect for the elderly was the value illustrated, the respondents wanted to save the 16-year and 45-year old men, perhaps believing those two could make greater contributions to society over time. The 70-year old Nobel prize winner, the respondents may have thought, had his day and his future contributions would be limited. Ordinarily the Korean people are prone to revere the elderly and respect their counsel. The Americans tend to favor young people, segregating themselves from older persons. In this case, the American value was supported, the Koreans foregoing their normal practice of valuing the elderly.

Although the American majority were inclined to provide some sort of solace to the situation five person who was apparently in ill-health, based on the American tendency to look after the well-being of others, not all of the American respondents were ready to give aid, contradictory to the typical American reaction. The reason may be that Americans are willing to help friends and neighbors in need, and are supporters of funding campaigns for the needy, and will con-tribute time and energy to worthy causes. Confronted, however, with a needy person in a face-to-face circumstance, they may be more reluctant to assist. The Koreans, this situations demonstrates, seem somewhat more willing to help those in need, especially when confronted almost directly.

Obeying parents is not a strong value among Americans or Koreans, although the Koreans may be slightly more respectful. Being with friends appears to hold sway over obedience, situation nine seems to imply.

Situation ten reflects somewhat the circumstances in situation nine — respect for family members. The responses indicate that a family reunion does not merit the consideration that being with friends does, although a large majority of Americans would try to do both. Friends may be more valued than family members.

In the other six situations, the majority stood together. Americans and Koreans favored the moral value in situation two, emotional restraint in three, equality in four, friendship in six, group-centeredness in seven, and honesty in eight. The six values were held in common by the two cultures.

Research on values comparing the United States and Korea is limited. The Ishii, Thomas, and Klopf (1993) study examines values in the United States, Korea, and Japan using the Value Word scale. American and Korean respondents to that scale agreed to four of the valued included in the Value Preference questionnaire, the instrument used in this research. Morality, respect for parents, honesty, and emotional display carried the same weight across the two cultures. However, five others listed on both instruments do not. The Value Word scale and the Value Preference questionnaire show different results on the value of group-centeredness, equality, respect for elders, work relationships, and the well-being of others.

Another study, using the Value Word scale (Thomas, Park, & Ishii, 1993), gives similar reactions by the Americans and Koreans who took part in that study with the respondents in the current research. The Americans and Koreans were in agreement on the values of group centeredness, morality, honesty emotional display, and the well-being of others. They differ, however, on equality and work relationships.

Representing a low degree of reliability, the Value Preference questionnaire requires further refinement. The results of this study, however, indicate what was stated earlier — values differ across cultures and they differ among the people of a culture in terms of salience.

Table 1. Comparison between American and Korean university students on the value preference questionnaire (percentages have been rounded.)

1)In shark-infested waters, three men are adrift on a slowly sinking life raft. Their combined weight is too much to keep the raft afloat. Each weighs about 175 pounds. If one jumps off, the raft will float and the remaining two will survive. One is a 16-year old honor student, the second a 45-year old nuclear physicist, and the third a 70-year old Nobel prize winner. Who should jump?

16-year old	45-year old	70-year old
A=4.0%	A=5.7%	A=89.7%
K=3.2%	*K=20.6%*	*K=76.1%*

Americans (M=2.86, SD=.45) significantly different than Koreans (M= 2.73, SD=.51)
[t= 2.7, p < .007]

2): Even though the applicant scored high on the university entrance examinations, he was not admitted. The boy's parents heard that a courtesy payment to the school admission officer usually results in admission. What should the parents do?

A=15.4%
K=18.3% Give the admission officer money
A=61.7%
K=63.8% Meet with the admission officer but give him nothing

A=22.9%

K=17.9%   Accept the school's decision not to enroll their son

No significant difference between Americans (M=2.07, SD=.62) and Koreans (M=2.00, SD=.60)

3)During the funeral of a family member, the relatives outwardly expressed their sorrow with much loud moaning and crying, hysterical emotion and weeping. How would you respond at the funeral of a loved one?

A=29.3%

K=29.8%   Outwardly express your sorrow

A=63.8%

K=58.7%   Show emotional restraint

A=6.9%

K=11.0%   Repress all emotional displays

No significant difference between Americans (M=1.78, SD=.56) and Koreans (M=1.83, SD=.65)

4)A mother of two boys is confronted by the youngest son. He says, "You favor my brother over me. You should treat us as equals. I'm just as good as he is." The mother replies, "He's older than you." What do you think?

A=93.1%

K=89.4%   The mother should treat the boys as equals

A=5.7%

K=6.9%   The mother should favor the older son

A=1.1%

K=3.2%   The mother should favor the younger son

No significant difference between Americans (M=1.08, SD=.31) and Koreans (M=1.45, SD=.47)

5) Walking along the street you see a person lying in the gutter. Dirty and ill-kept, the person does not appear healthy. What would you do?

> A=38.9%
> *K=27.5%* Ignore the person
> A=38.9%
> *K=36.7%* Ask her if she needs help
> A=22.3%
> *K=35.8%* Give the help she requires

Americans (M=1.83, SD=.77) significantly different than Koreans (M= 2.10, SD=.81)
[t=3.31, p < .001]

6) The work day ends and you are ready to quit work and have some fun. You need company. Who do you ask to join you?

> A=5.7%
> *K=17.0%* Your fellow workers
> A=42.3%
> *K=31.2%* Your fellow workers and selected friends
> A=52.0%
> *K=51.8%* Your special friends

No significant difference between Americans (M=2.46, SD=.60) and Koreans (M=2.35, SD=.75)

7) You have two hours to prepare for an examination and a report you and several fellow students have to give. The report earns a group grade; the exam score is your own. In the two hours you can do

only one well. What should you do?

A=18.3%
K=22.5%   Study for the test, not the group report
A=8.0%
K=9.6%   Prepare for the group report, not the test
A=73.7%
K=67.9%   Try to do both

No significant difference between Americans (M=2.55, SD=.79) and Koreans (M=2.45, SD=.84)

8)Poverty-stricken, you make only $100 per week, hardly enough to take care of your sick wife and crippled child. Walking along the street you find $5,000 in an envelope with a man's name on it. What should you do?

A=50.0%
K=47.2%   Return the money
A=47.1%
K=45.0%   Use the money for your wife and child
A=2.9%
K=7.3%   Keep the money and do not tell your wife and child

No significant difference between Americans (M=1.53, SD=.56) and Koreans (M=1.61, SD=.64)

9)Susan's parents are spending the weekend visiting relatives in a distant city. Susan is told to keep the house clean and hold no parties. Susan's friends pressure her to have a wild party. What should she do?

A=14.5%

K=13.4% Hold the party
A=36.0%
K=44.2% Obey her parents
A=49.4%
K=41.9% Compromise and just have several friends over

Americans (M=2.35, SD=.72) significantly different than Koreans (M= 2.71, SD=.59)
[t=5.46, p < .001]

10) Your parents want you to attend a family reunion. Three friends who you have not seen for months call and want you to go out with them. They are in town for that day only. What should you do?

A=9.8%
K=13.4% Go with your parents
A=17.8%
K=44.2% Go with your friends
A=72.4%
K=41.9% Try to do both

Americans (M=2.63, SD=.66) significantly different than Koreans (M= 2.30, SD=.71)
[t=4.67, p < .001]

REFERENCES

Ishii, S. and Klopf, K. (1989). Human Values in Intercultural Communication: Japan Compared to the U.S.A. Otsuma Review, 21.

Klopf, D.W. (1991). Intercultural Encounters. Englewood, CO:Morton.

7. COMMUNICATION PRACTICES IN KOREA*

Myung-seok Park
Moon-soo Kim
Dankook University

* Communication Quarterly, Vol. 40, No. 4, Fall 1992, Pages 398-404

The communication practices of Koreans are explored which are divergent from those employed elsewhere in the world. Distinction in social behavior impinging on communication include Confucianistic ethics, filial piety, age, gender, and hierarchical structure. Verbal and nonverbal differences relate to maintaining harmony in interpersonal relationships. The essay concludes with analyses from six research reports, comparing Korean communication styles to those in other cultures.

KEY CONCEPTS Confucianism, age, gender, filial piety, harmony, verbal behavior, nonverbal behavior, argumentativeness, assertiveness, responsiveness, aggressiveness, communication apprehension, interpersonal need satisfaction, loneliness.

An American teaching in Korea writes about cultural differences in Korean and American communication in the following:

> On a few occasions I have found myself somewhat angered when Koreans barged in to where I was sitting, seemingly oblivious to the fact of my privacy. After discussing this with my Korean co-workers, I realized that the Korean custom is to cough before entering a room as opposed to knocking. On each of the interruptions of my privacy there was the sound of coughing before the door flew open. Knowing the Korean custom I now see the truth of the situation. As an American I had been angry because the people did not have the courtesy to knock, and in retrospect I see that they did "knock," at least in the usual manner of their country (Comerford, 1979).

A minor communication difference, the custom of coughing instead of knocking, obviously upset the American and likely the Koreans confronted by his irritation. To Koreans the cough is a subtle and quiet expression of warning — an indirect, warm suggestion. Koreans see knocking as a direct and overt expression of caution often startling to someone. Knocking disturbs and annoys Koreans, and represents a loss of etiquette. Coughing is just one of the cultural practices illustrating that taboos and beliefs in one culture could be interpreted differently in another, resulting in mutual misunderstandings.

In this essay practices considered customary in Korea will be explored with the intent of revealing distinctions between those practices that impinge on communication in Korea and in other cultures around the world.

SOCIAL BEHAVIOR

To Americans the interpersonal behavior of Koreans in the presence of family, work associates, or friends may seem strange. The basic concepts and codes of Confucian ethics run deep in the thinking of Korean people. The Confucian way governs most interpersonal interaction. Its basic premise is that proper human relationships are the foundation of society. Proper interpersonal relations include warm feelings between people, or humanism, placing the relationship before personal interests, or faithfulness; and respect for ritual and proper form, or propriety. Koreans attend to group welfare and harmony. But Korea's long history of violence taught Koreans to survive, and sometime at the expense of harmony, pragmatics will rule. Koreans have placated occupying powers to endure.

Throughout Korea's conflict-riddled history, Koreans aligned with their most immediate groups-families. Kinships will take priority over other group affiliations. And, it is in the family where differences between Koreans and Americans are apparent.

Although the family unit is shifting from husband, wife and many children to a husband, wife, and one or two children, and as women gradually are claiming status and rights equal to men, the old relationships prevail. Passions are not freely and openly expressed; love is not as warm and sweet as in the United States. Korean wives do not rush to embrace their husbands at airports or train stations even though the men were away for years. The love is inward with passionate expressions surpressed. Koreans are more reserved than Americans.

In the company of their elders, young people do not smoke or drink. Impolite also is the wearing of glasses in the presence of elders or at funerals. Belching, hawing, or hiccoughing is permissible at the dinner table, although blowing the nose is not. Talking is usually avoided until the meal is finished, and food is not touched with the hands, only with chopsticks, spoons, or forks.

Sons are preferred to continue the patrilineal succession from father to son. Sons are accorded more love, given more toys, clothing, and bedding than the daughters. Son-less mothers are humiliated and maltreated.

Filial piety, along with the father-son relationship, is of utmost importance in all family relations. The children are absolutely obedient to their parents, serving them and pleasing them not only during the parent's lifetime, but even after death. The son has the duty of taking care of his parents in their old age and, after their death, he has the responsibility of performing family memorial rites according to Confucian custom.

Koreans on occasion believe it to be to their advantage to look or be older than their associates. Old age bestows much respectability, and in some circumstances individuals may add a year or two to their age to gain an edge.

To Koreans, growing old represents signs of grace, respect, and piety, and age is the first consideration when Koreans communicate with one another. Old age is always venerated, and different language honorifics and different mental attitudes are employed with the elders in communicative interactions. Foreigners wanting to communicate effectively with Koreans must take age into consideration. The older the Korean, the more respect is given. Even in exchanging business cards, care must be practiced when meeting an older Korean. Two hands hold the card as it is extended, one hand a bit behind the other.

In family relationships Koreans and Americans follow divergent paths as they do in other areas of interpersonal relationships. In Korea all human relations are affected by a consideration of others. Personal and emotional relationships underlie the culture's structure. Face-saving is crucial, and a Korean would not want to be responsible for causing shame for someone because of his or her actions.

Showing favors to friends or school alumni is common and typical

Koreans make sacrifices to help their friends in whatever way possible. If asked for a favor, the Korean must respond regardless of reason or common sense. The idea of total friendship may seem stifling to Americans. To Koreans, Americans with their individualistic ways often seem cold and unfriendly.

Confucian ethics control interpersonal relationships. One is always more powerful than the other. One is always lower in rank than the other. A person's respect and loyalty toward someone older or higher in rank is absolute. Persons who break the rule are considered rude. Human relationships are always vertical in every facet of Korean life. The concept of equality hardly exists in everyday interactions.

Toward outgroup members or strangers, Koreans are apt to be indifferent. Strangers are met with fixed and rigid faces, which will melt into soft, warm, and smiling expressions when friends approach. Within their own groups, Koreans are friendly and courteous—quite different than the dead-pan features strangers see.

VERBAL AND NONVERBAL BEHAVIOR

Misunderstandings in intercultural communication situations generally can be attributed to the verbal and nonverbal communicative patterns of the communicators. Important as a communicative medium is verbal behavior or language, but a shrug of the shoulders, a nod, a wink, or a thumbs-down movement contribute greatly to understanding. Distinctive qualities of Korean verbal and nonverbal often cause misunderstandings in intercultural interactions.

Koreans use "yes" in linguistic contexts whereas Americans say "no." When a Korean is asked, "Didn't you go to school yesterday?" he will invariably answer "Yes, I didn't." An American would reply, "No, I didn't." The Korean's "yes" indicates agreement with the inquirer's assumption that the respondent did not go to school.

The Koreans use "yes" in different ways than Americans. When a Korean is asked, "How are you?" he is inclined to answer, "Yes, I'm fine. Thank you. And you?" "Yes" in this case is a sign of recognition of the question asked. But the Korean answer "yes" does not always indicate agreement. Usually the Korean "yes" means "I fully understand what you are talking about; please continue." The Korean "yes" does not necessarily mean agreement or intention of complying. More often the "yes" means understanding, not agreement. Misunderstandings will arise if foreigners take the Korean "yes" as consent.

Koreans are "yes" directed in order to avoid being negative in communication situations. The feelings of the listener are always taken into account and the speaker chooses words that will not hurt the listener's feelings. The harmony of the interaction could be disturbed with a "no" reply. What is important is not the correctness of an answer, but the maintenance of interpersonal goodwill.

In interpersonal communication situations, Koreans are careful about showing proper respect for the feelings and sensitivities of others. Maintaining the other person's "kibun," the person's "face" or self-esteem requires attention to the state of the listeners' inner feelings. The wise Korean is quick to understand the listeners' "kibun," making them feel like a million dollars rather than like eating worms.

This type of affective communication in which the feelings of the listeners are stressed can bring about intercultural misunderstandings. For the sake of living in harmony, Koreans tend to do everything to avoid appearing to oppose anyone directly. Koreans in intercultural situations often come across as seemingly agreeing with their foreigner communicators when in reality they are merely showing sympathy for the foreigner's position. A statement such as "I understand the position you are in, and I'll do my best," while accepted by the foreigner as a commitment, often is a polite way of saying, "I cannot do it." Americans, for example, are prone to draw heavily on the words said without considering the silent assumptions upon which the words are based.

The American patterns which place emphasis on getting the message across can aptly be called the "instrumental" communication style. In this pattern, verbally expressed messages play an important role. The Koreans, and, for that matter, the Japanese, use an "affective" or "situation-based" communication style in which non-linguistic elements such as feelings and attitudes play an important role. The instrumental communication style places the stress on ideas or thoughts while the affective style emphasizes the communication of feelings. Many of the American problems in its relations with Japan stem from the American inability to recognize and deal with the affective style practiced by the Japanese. In face-to-face discussions, the Japanese are thought to be agreeing or committing themselves to an American point of view when the Japanese are only attempting to maintain harmonious relations and are not agreeing to anything. The Americans return home elated with their success and the Japanese are telling the folks at home no agreement was reached. Americans then are preplexed by the change of heart of the Japanese and want to boycott Japanese imports. The Japanese question the intelligence of their American counterparts. Both sides could benefit from courses in intercultural communication!

The contrast between the instrumental style of the Americans and the Korean affective style is striking. The Americans assert themselves or make themselves understood by talking. Korean people defend themselves by vague expressions or not talking. Americans try to persuade their listeners in a step-by-step process whether or not the listeners accept them totally. But a Korean is apt to refuse to talk further with a person whose attitude the speaker cannot accept, or the totality of that person's thinking and feeling.

When Koreans are involved in business transactions, they approach the persons they want to converse with by way of an introduction through mutual friends. Once a human relationship is established, they convey their messages through the channel of food and drink — an indirect-intermediated communication process. Americans, in contrast, attempt to solve problems through direct, face-to-face contact, motivated by a self-assertive attitude. Americans put sincerity and directness before harmony.

Instead of getting directly to the point, Koreans tend to engage in long descriptive accounts about a person or event in subjective terms. They probably will not answer questions directly when asked. Data or other forms of evidence are not given to prove a point. Talk is not a game of logic but is an emotional exchange.

Nonverbally, the Korean culture is like most other cultures, attaching its own set of meanings to nonverbal acts. The "come here" gesture, for example, is the arm extended outward, palm down, with the fingers fluttered several times. The raised middle finger is used for pointing occasionally and carries no sexual connotation. But a thumb inserted between the second and middle fingers of the same hand holds the same sexual implication as the gesturing middle finger in the United States.

Many idiomatic expressions are connected to nonverbal behavior. In Korean "her hand is big" means the same as the English "she is generous with her money"; "her eyes are high, and won't marry a nobody" means "she aims high, and won't marry a bum"; "his nose is high" means "he is snooty"; "the robber contaminated the house with the poison of his eyes" means "the robber marked the house for burglary."

Hawing and belching at meal time implies the diner enjoyed the meal, the cook should be complimented. Traditionally, a husband and wife walking side by side is taboo; the woman follows several steps behind the man. Koreans laugh or giggle where Americans would frown or be dead serious. Koreans smile when trying to conceal anguish or enmity. Making a circle with the thumb and second finger means "money" in Korea, and OK in the United States. Thumbs up is "number one," "boss," or "best" in Korea; in America it signifies OK. Flexing one's arms and raising the hands above the shoulders would be construed as a threat, but in America it is seen as an expression of strength. Raising a finger to the mouth and hissing "shhhhh" means a child wants to perform before the toilet; in America the same sound and gesture means to be quiet. A man pointing to the reproductive organs suggests he is strong and ready to work hard.

COMPARISONS BETWEEN KOREA AND OTHER CULTURES

In this final section, research is reported which reveals characteristics about Korean communicative behavior as it relates to that in other cultures, particularly the United States. The Korean subject-participants for the most part are university students who attend school in Seoul.

ARGUMENTATIVENESS

Argumentativeness is a personality trait which contains tendencies to approach and avoid arguments. Persons with approach tendencies will advocate positions on controversial issues and attack conflicting positions. Those with avoidance tendencies try to stay out of arguments but, if forced to do so, will feel uncomfortable arguing. The approach types (high argumentatives) perceive argument as an exciting challenge. The avoidance types (low argumentatives) feel relieved when they are able to avoid an argument.

Jenkins, Klopf and Park (1991) compared Koreans and Americans using the Infante/ Rancer Argumentativeness Scale to measure their tendencies to approach and avoid arguments. The results show a significant difference between the Koreans and Americans to approach arguments, no significant difference between the two groups on the tendency to avoid arguments, and a significant difference between the Koreans and the Americans on the degree of argumentativeness. The Americans are more argumentatively inclined than are the Koreans, perceiving arguments as stimulating competition. Neither group, however, could be perceived as being highly argumentative even though the Americans are more willing to argue.

ASSERTIVENESS/RESPONSIVENESS

Assertiveness is a person's ability to state opinions with conviction and defend them against personal attack. It relates to a person's skill in making requests, actively disagreeing with someone else, expressing positive or negative feelings, initiating, maintaining, and disengaging from conversations without attacking others. Assertive persons are able to maintain their self respect, satisfy personal needs, pursue personal happiness, and defend their rights without affecting the rights of others.

Responsiveness concerns a person's sensitivity to the feelings of others as these are verbalized. Being responsive a person is a good listener, is able to make others comfortable in speaking situations, is aware of the needs of others, is helpful, sympathetic, warm and understanding, is open as a communicator, and responsive to the rights of others without forfeiting his or her own.

Sallinen-Kuparinen, Thompson, Ishii, Park and Klopf (1991) compared assertiveness and responsiveness across several cultures using the McCroskey/Richmond Assertiveness/ Responsiveness Measure. The results on the assertiveness dimension of the measure show the Americans to be significantly more assertive than the Koreans, Finns, and Japanese, and the Koreans significantly more assertive than the Finns and Japanese. On the responsiveness dimension, no significant difference occurred between the Americans and Koreans, but a significant difference did appear between the Americans and the Finns and Japanese and between the Koreans and the Finns and Japanese.

For the Koreans, the assertiveness/responsiveness study indicates that the Koreans are highly assertive and more so than the Finns and Japanese, but not as much as the Americans. The Koreans, like the Americans, are more responsive to the talk of others than the Finns and Japanese, being good listeners while making others comfortable in speaking situations (Park and Klopf, 1992).

AGGRESSIVENESS

The threat or infliction of physical or psychological pain or damage between conspecifics is aggression, a personality trait which can be found in most animal species. Among human beings aggression may be physical or verbal.

Scheel, Klopf and Park(1991) analyzed the verbal aggressiveness of Koreans, comparing them to Americans using the Verbal Aggressiveness Scale. The Koreans were significantly more aggressive than the Americans (Park and Klopf, 1992).

COMMUNICATION APPREHENSION

Communication apprehension is a person's level of fear or anxiety associated with either real or anticipated talk with one or more persons. Park, Klopf, and Cambra (1978) investigated the prevalence of communication apprehension among Koreans, Americans, Australians, and Japanese. The results reveal the Koreans to be less apprehensive in oral communication situations than the others.

INTERPERSONAL NEED SATISFACTION

According to many theories of motivation, people behave as they do in order to satisfy certain needs, desires, or wants. Some of these needs can be satisfied only in the company of other people and these needs and interpersonal communication are fundamentally interdependent. Communication is the medium through which these needs are satisfied.

The FIRO-B inventory measures three of these needs — inclusion, control, and affection. Inclusion is the need to be accepted, understood, and listened to. Control is the need to control others, be in charge, or make decisions. Affection is the need to have close personal relations with others or the capacity to want love.

Koreans were compared to Americans, Australians, and Japanese with the FIRO-B (Park, Cambra, and Klopf, 1979). For inclusion, the Koreans were significantly more satisfied than the Americans and Australians but not as significantly satisfied as the Japanese. For control, the Koreans had a significantly stronger need to control in interpersonal relations than the other three groups. For affection, the Koreans were not significantly different than the Americans and Australians, but the Japanese were significantly more satisfied than the other three groups.

LONELINESS

The inability to talk with others is a major factor in loneliness. Passive, apprehensive, or shy persons are likely to exhibit loneliness as they are apt to be communicatively incompetent.

Simmons, Klopf, and Park (1991) assessed the loneliness of Koreans and Americans using the Differential Loneliness Scale. The Koreans proved to be significantly more lonely than the Americans. The higher degree of loneliness among the Koreans probably can be attributed to the Korean need to be in the company of others, especially friends and relatives. The participants in the study, freshmen at college, were away from home for the first time and away from friends and family who were to some degree in their presence (Park and Klopf, 1992).

CONCLUSION

It is obvious that Korean patterns of communicative behavior are different than other cultures, especially the United States — close friends and allies. The differences, however, are found largely in superficial customs and attitudes. In every culture people experience similar emotions, share similar dreams and ambitions for themselves and their children, and desire similar comforts and knowledge which make life worth living. Although strangers often find difficulties in muddling their way through these superficial differences to get at the real core all human beings share, it is possible with determination and cultural sensitivity. Once strangers have mastered the language and thought patterns of a new country, no matter how different from their own, the strangers will uncover a great deal of satisfaction in their communicative relationships with the people of that country. They will be much better persons for the added knowledge and experiences that country can provide.

REFERENCES

Comerford, J. A. (1979). Introduction. In M-S Park, *Communication Styles in Two Different Cultures: Korean and American.* Seoul: Han Shin.

Jenkins, G., Klopf, D. W. & Park, M-S (1991). Argumentativeness in Korean and American College Students. Paper presented at the World Communication Association convention, Jyvaskyla, Finland.

Park, M-S (1979). *Communication Styles in Two different Cultures: Korean and American.* Seoul: Han Shin.

Park, M-S, Cambra, R. E. & Klopf, D. W. (1979). Characteristics of Korean Oral Communication Practices. *Korea Journal, 19,* 4-8.

Park, M-S & Klopf, D. W. (1992). Characteristics of Korean Communication. *Korea Journal,* in press.

Park, M-S, Klopf, D. W. & Cambra, R. E. (1978). A Comparison of the Prevalence of Communication Apprehension in Korea, America, Australia, and Japan. *Korea Journal, 18,* 33-38.

Sallinen-Kuparinen, A., Thompson, C. A., Ishii, S., Park, M-S, & Klopf, D. W. (1991). An Analysis of Social Style among Disparate Cultures. Paper presented at the World Communication Association Convention, Jyvaskyla, Finland.

Scheel, J., Park, M-S, & Klopf, D. W. (1991). A Comparison of Verbal Aggressiveness among Koreans and Americans. Paper submitted for publication.

Simmons, C., Klopf, D. W. & Park, M-S (1991). Loneliness among Korean and American University Students. *Psychological Reports, 68,* 754.

BIBLIOGRAPHY

Adler, Mortimer J. 1970. *The Time of Our Lives: The Ethics of Common Sense.* New York: Holt, Rinehart, and Winston, pp. 122-123.

Berlin, B. and Kay, P. 1969. *Basic Color Terms.* Berkeley and Los Angeles: University of California Press.

Boorstin, Daniel J. 1960. *America and the Image of Europe: Reflections on American Thought.* Cleveland: The World Publishing Company.

Boucher, Jerry D. 1974. "Display Rules and Facial Affective Behavior: A Theoretical Discussion and Suggestions for Research." In *Topics in Culture Learning,* Vol. 2, ed. Richard W. Brislin. Honolulu: East-West Center Press. pp. 87-102.

____. 1974. "Culture and the Expression of Emotion." *International and Intercultural Communication Annual.* Published by the Speech Communication Association, Statler-Hilton Hotel, New York N.Y.

Caroll, John B. 1955. *The Study of Language.* Cambridge: Harvard University Press.

Catford, J. C. 1965. *A Linguistic Theory of Translation.* London: Oxford University Press.

Chang, Wang-Rock. 1973. "Pitfalls of Translation." In Papers to Honor Professor C. D. Pi on His Sixty-First Birthday. Seoul: Samhwa Publishing Company, pp. 39-44.

Choi, Synduck. 1975. "Social Change and the Korean Family." *Korea Journal* Vol. 15, No. 11, pp. 4-13.

Chomsky, Noam. 1965. *Aspects of the Theory of Syntax.* Cambridge, Mass.: The M.I.T. Press.

Condon, John C., and Yousef, Fathi S. 1976. *An Introduction to Intercultural Communication.* Indianapolis: The Bobbs-Merrill Company, Inc.

Crane, Paul S. 1967. *Korean Patterns.* Seoul: Hollym Corporation. (Royal Asiatic Society, Korea Branch Handbook Series Number 1).

Deese, James. 1965. *The Structure of Associations in Language and Thought.* Baltimore: The Johns Hopkins Press.

Doi, L. Takeo. 1956. "Japanese Language as an Expression of Japanese Psychology." *Western Speech,* Vol. 20, pp. 90-96.

Dredge, C. Paul. 1976. "Social Rules of Speech in Korean: The Views of a Comic Strip Character." *Korea Journal* Vol. 16, No. 1, pp. 4-14.

Ekman, Paul, ed. 1973. *Darwin and Facial Expression.* New York: Academic Press.

Glenn, Edmund S. 1966. *Mind, Culture, Politics. Mimeographed.*

____. 1954. "Semantic Difficulties in International Communication." *ETC.,* Vol. 11, No.3, pp. 163-180.

Ha, Hyong-Kang. 1975. "Preference for Male Issue in Korean History." *Korea Journal* Vol.15, No. 6, pp. 44-53.

Hall, Edward T. 1959. *The Silent Language.* New York: Doubleday.

Hayakawa, S. I. 1939. *Language in Thought and Action.* New York: Harcourt, Brace

& World, Inc.

Henry, Jules. 1963. *Culture against Man*. New York: Random House.

Hwang, Juck-Ryoon. 1975. *Role of Sociolinguistics in Foreign Language Education with Reference to Korean and English Terms of Address and Levels of Deference*. Seoul: Tap Publishing Company, pp. 20-22.

Kim, Inseok. 1989. Korean Language as Pragmatic-based Discourse. *Korean Language Education* (Vol. 1) pp.12-24.

____ , 1990. Typological Characteristics of the English and Korean Languages: Mirror-image Phenomenon. *Applied Linguistics of Korea* (Vol. 4). pp. 23-56.

____ , 1990. *A Collection of Curious Expressions and Proverbs of English*. Seoul: Si-sa-young-a-sa.

Kim, Ki-hong. 1975. "Cross-Cultural Differences Between Americans and Koreans in Nonverbal Behavior." In *The Korean Language: Its Structure and Social Projection*, ed. Ho-Min Sohn. Honolulu: The Center for Korean Studies/University of Hawaii, pp. 5-18.

Kluckhohn, Clyde. 1954. "American Culture—A General Description." In *Human Factors in Military Operations*, ed. Richard H. Williams, Technical Memorandum ORO-T-259, Operations Research Office. Chevy Chase, Maryland: The Johns Hopkins University, pp. 92-111.

Kluckhohn, Florence R. and Strodtbeck, Fred L. 1961. *Variations in Value Orientations*. New York: Row, Peterson.

La Barre, Weston. 1976. "Paralinguistics, Kinesics, and Cultural Anthropology." In *Inter-Cultural Communication: A Reader*, eds. Larry A. Samovar and Richard E. Porter, 2nd ed. Belmont California: Wadsworth Publishing Company, Inc., pp. 221-29.

Lee, Grant S. 1976. "The Confucian Weltanschauung: An Extension of Filial Axis." *Korea Journal* Vol. 16, No. 4, pp. 21-6.

Lee, O-Young. 1967. *In This Earth & In That Wind: This is Korea*. Trans. by David I. Steinberg. Seoul: Hollym Corp.

Leech, G. 1990. *Semantics*: The Study of Meaning. London: Penguin.

Lin, Yutang. 1972. "On Growing Old Gracefully." *Readings in English*. Seoul: Seoul National University Press, pp. 61-71.

Lukoff, Fred. 1963. "English Phonological Pitfalls." *The English Language and Literature*. Seoul: The English Literary Society of Korea, Vol. 14, p. 10.

Lyons, J. 1977. Semantics. (Vol. 1). Cambridge: Cambridge University Press.

Nakamura Hajime. 1969. *Ways of Thinking of Eastern Peoples: India, China, Tibet, Japan*. Honolulu: East-West Center Press.

Nida, Eugene A. 1969. "Science of Translation." Language 45, pp. 483-498.

Osgood, Charles. E., May, William H., and Miron, Murray S. 1975. *Cross-Cultural Universals of Affective Meaning*. Chicago: University of Illinois Press.

Park, Myung-seok. 1973. "English-Korean, Korean-English Simultaneous Interpretation." (in Korean) *Language and Linguistics*. Seoul: Hankuk University of Foreign Studies, pp. 42-65.

Park, Soon-ham. 1975. "On Special Uses of Kinship Terms in Korean." *Korea Journal* Vol. 15, No. 9, pp. 4-8.

Potter, David M. 1954. People of Plenty: *Economic Abundance and the American*

Character. Chicago: The University of Chicago Press.

Prator, Clifford H, Jr. 1957. *Manual of American English Pronunciation.* New York: Holt, Rinehart and Winston.

Quine, Willard V. 1964. "Meaning and Translation." In *The Structure of Language: Readings in the Philosophy of Language,* eds. Jerry A. Fodor and Jerrold J. Katz. Englewood Cliffs, New Jersey: Prentice-Hall, pp. 460-478.

Radhakrishnan, S. 1962. "The Indian Approach to the Religious Problem." In *Philosophy and Culture, East and West,* ed. Charles A. Moore. Honolulu: University of Hawaii Press, p. 255.

Reischauer, Edwin O., and Fairbank, John K. 1958. *East Asia, The Great Tradition,* Vol. 1. Boston: Houghton Mifflin Co.

Rutt, Richard. 1966. "The Translation of Korean Literature: Problems and Achievements." In Papers to Honor Professor Ha-Yoon Lee on His Sixtieth Birthday. Seoul, pp. 141-164.

Song, Yo-in. 1969. "Literary Translation: A Linguistic Overview." *Dongguk Journal.* Seoul: Dongguk University, Vol. 6 pp. 16-32.

____. 1972. "On Englishing Korean Prose; A Linguistic Inquiry." (in Korean) *The English Language and Literature.* Seoul: The English Literary Society of Korea, Vol. 42, pp. 33-53.

____. 1975. Translation: *Theory and Practice.* Seoul: Dongguk University Press.

____. 1976. "Some Implications of Weltanschaung in Translation Theory with Special Reference to English and Korean." *Linguistic Journal of Korea.* Seoul: The Linguistic Society of Korea, pp. 89-177.

Stageberg, Norman C. 1965. *An Introductory English Grammar.* New York: Holt, Rinehart and Winston, Inc.

Stewart, Edward C. 1972. *American Cultural Patterns: A Cross-Cultural Perspective.* Dimensions of International Education, No. 3. Pittsburgh, Pennsylvania: University of Pittsburgh Press.

Takeyama, Yasuo. 1972. *Fukurodataki no Nippon* (Beaten-up Japan). Tokyo: The Simul Press, Inc.

Trudgill, Peter. 1974. *Sociolinguistics: An Introduction.* London: Penguin.

Ueda, Keiko. 1972. "Sixteen Ways to Avoid Saying "No" in Japan: A Survey of the Function and Frequency of Japanese Patterns of Declining Requests." The Paper was presented at the Conference on Communication Across Cultures: Contact and Conflict, I.C.U., Tokyo, July 9-17.

Walsh, John E. 1913. *Intercultural Education in the Community of Man* (An East West Center Book) Honolulu: The University of Hawaii Press.

Williams, Robin M., Jr. 1961. *American Society: A Sociological Interpretation.* New York: Alfred A. Knopf, pp. 415-426.

Yoon, Jong-joo. 1971. *A Study on Fertility and Out-migration in A Rural Area.* Seoul: Seoul Women's College Press.

Yoshikawa, Muneo. 1974. "Psycho-Sociological Implications of the Japanese Interpersonal Communication Patterns." In the Third Summer Program in East West Intercultural Studies (July 21- August 11, 1914).

INDEX